VOLUME 181

Eritrea

Randall Fegley

Compiler

D0169012

CLIO PRESS

OXFORD, ENGLAND · SANTA BARBARA, CALIFORNIA
DENVER, COLORADO

© Copyright 1995 by ABC-CLIO Ltd.

British Library Cataloguing in Publication Data

Eritrea – (World Bibliographical Series;
Vol. 181)
I. Fegley, Randall.   II. Series
016.9635

ISBN 1–85109–245–5

ABC-CLIO Ltd.,
Old Clarendon Ironworks,
35A Great Clarendon Street,
Oxford OX2 6AT, England.

ABC-CLIO Inc.,
130 Cremona Drive,
Santa Barbara,
CA 93116, USA.

Designed by Bernard Crossland.
Typeset by Columns Design and Production Services Ltd., Reading, England.
Printed and bound in Great Britain by Bookcraft (Bath) Ltd., Midsomer Norton.

Eritrea

WORLD BIBLIOGRAPHICAL SERIES

General Editors:
Robert G. Neville (Executive Editor)
John J. Horton

Robert A. Myers   Hans H. Wellisch
Ian Wallace   Ralph Lee Woodward, Jr.

John J. Horton is Deputy Librarian of the University of Bradford and currently Chairman of its Academic Board of Studies in Social Sciences. He has maintained a longstanding interest in the discipline of area studies and its associated bibliographical problems, with special reference to European Studies. In particular he has published in the field of Icelandic and of Yugoslav studies, including the two relevant volumes in the World Bibliographical Series.

Robert A. Myers is Associate Professor of Anthropology in the Division of Social Sciences and Director of Study Abroad Programs at Alfred University, Alfred, New York. He has studied post-colonial island nations of the Caribbean and has spent two years in Nigeria on a Fulbright Lectureship. His interests include international public health, historical anthropology and developing societies. In addition to *Amerindians of the Lesser Antilles: a bibliography* (1981), *A Resource Guide to Dominica, 1493-1986* (1987) and numerous articles, he has compiled the World Bibliographical Series volumes on *Dominica* (1987), *Nigeria* (1989) and *Ghana* (1991).

Ian Wallace is Professor of German at the University of Bath. A graduate of Oxford in French and German, he also studied in Tübingen, Heidelberg and Lausanne before taking teaching posts at universities in the USA, Scotland and England. He specializes in contemporary German affairs, especially literature and culture, on which he has published numerous articles and books. In 1979 he founded the journal *GDR Monitor*, which he continues to edit under its new title *German Monitor*.

Hans H. Wellisch is Professor emeritus at the College of Library and Information Services, University of Maryland. He was President of the American Society of Indexers and was a member of the International Federation for Documentation. He is the author of numerous articles and several books on indexing and abstracting, and has published *The Conversion of Scripts and Indexing and Abstracting: an International Bibliography*, and *Indexing from A to Z*. He also contributes frequently to *Journal of the American Society for Information Science*, *The Indexer* and other professional journals.

Ralph Lee Woodward, Jr. is Professor of History at Tulane University, New Orleans. He is the author of *Central America, a Nation Divided*, 2nd ed. (1985), as well as several monographs and more than seventy scholarly articles on modern Latin America. He has also compiled volumes in the World Bibliographical Series on *Belize* (1980), *El Salvador* (1988), *Guatemala* (Rev. Ed.) (1992) and *Nicaragua* (Rev. Ed.) (1994). Dr. Woodward edited the Central American section of the *Research Guide to Central America and the Caribbean* (1985) and is currently associate editor of Scribner's *Encyclopedia of Latin American History*.

THE WORLD BIBLIOGRAPHICAL SERIES

This series, which is principally designed for the English speaker, will eventually cover every country (and many of the world's principal regions), each in a separate volume comprising annotated entries on works dealing with its history, geography, economy and politics; and with its people, their culture, customs, religion and social organization. Attention will also be paid to current living conditions – housing, education, newspapers, clothing, etc. – that are all too often ignored in standard bibliographies; and to those particular aspects relevant to individual countries. Each volume seeks to achieve, by use of careful selectivity and critical assessment of the literature, an expression of the country and an appreciation of its nature and national aspirations, to guide the reader towards an understanding of its importance. The keynote of the series is to provide, in a uniform format, an interpretation of each country that will express its culture, its place in the world, and the qualities and background that make it unique. The views expressed in individual volumes, however, are not necessarily those of the publisher.

VOLUMES IN THE SERIES

1 *Yugoslavia*, Rev. Ed., John J. Horton
2 *Lebanon*, Rev. Ed., C. H. Bleaney
3 *Lesotho*, Shelagh M. Willet and David Ambrose
4 *Zimbabwe*, Rev. Ed., Deborah Potts
5 *Saudi Arabia*, Rev. Ed., Frank A. Clements
6 *Russia/USSR*, Second Ed., Lesley Pitman
7 *South Africa*, Rev. Ed., Geoffrey V. Davis
8 *Malawi*, Rev. Ed., Samuel Decalo
9 *Guatemala*, Rev. Ed., Ralph Lee Woodward, Jr.
10 *Pakistan*, David Taylor
11 *Uganda*, Robert L. Collison
12 *Malaysia*, Ian Brown and Rajeswary Ampalavanar
13 *France*, Rev. Ed., Frances Chambers
14 *Panama*, Eleanor DeSelms Langstaff
15 *Hungary*, Thomas Kabdebo
16 *USA*, Sheila R. Herstein and Naomi Robbins
17 *Greece*, Richard Clogg and Mary Jo Clogg
18 *New Zealand*, R. F. Grover

19 *Algeria*, Richard I. Lawless
20 *Sri Lanka*, Vijaya Samaraweera
21 *Belize*, Second Ed., Peggy Wright and Brian E. Coutts
23 *Luxembourg*, Carlo Hury and Jul Christophory
24 *Swaziland*, Rev. Ed., Balam Nyeko
25 *Kenya*, Robert L. Collison
26 *India*, Rev. Ed., Ian Derbyshire
27 *Turkey*, Merel Güçlü
28 *Cyprus*, Rev. Ed., P. M. Kitromilides and M. L. Evriviades
29 *Oman*, Rev. Ed., Frank A. Clements
30 *Italy*, Lucio Sponza and Diego Zancani
31 *Finland*, J. E. O. Screen
32 *Poland*, Rev. Ed., George Sanford and Adriana Gozdecka-Sanford
33 *Tunisia*, Allan M. Findlay, Anne M. Findlay and Richard I. Lawless
34 *Scotland*, Eric G. Grant
35 *China*, Peter Cheng
36 *Qatar*, P. T. H. Unwin
37 *Iceland*, John J. Horton
38 *Nepal*, John Whelpton
39 *Haiti*, Rev. Ed., Frances Chambers
40 *Sudan*, Rev. Ed., M. W. Daly

Contents

Contents

Contents

Preface

As Africa's most recently established nation, Eritrea presents a new field of study for scholars. Although a surprising amount has been written on the country, there is a lack of significant reference works in certain areas. Hence the general aim of this bibliography is to present Eritrea in its many facets to the English-speaking world. Items have been selected for their importance, authority, variety and accessibility and priority has been given to sources in English. Some important Italian and other European-language works have also been included, however, since Italian sources, though frequently dated, are numerous and often very thorough. No bibliography of Eritrea would be complete without them.

Another consideration when choosing entries was the particular importance of certain fields. For example, important studies in modern and contemporary history, ethnology, and religion have been conducted in the country and therefore these sections of the bibliography contain a relatively large number of entries. In addition, special attention has also been paid to areas such as politics and economics and these sections have been lengthened accordingly. Recent works in some important fields have been included for their value as updates to other older material. Finally, it would not be possible to compile a comprehensive reference work on Eritrea without including numerous sources from Ethiopia. Hence throughout this work, various sources from and/or on Ethiopia have been used where they apply to Eritrea, particularly in cases of literature relevant to the eras when Eritrean and Ethiopian history and culture have converged.

Indeed one of the difficulties in compiling this work has been that of separating Ethiopia and Eritrea, since a substantial knowledge of Ethiopia is required of anyone studying Eritrea in its own right. The most noteworthy books have been listed as entries, while articles and other important, but secondary, sources have been incorporated into other entries.

Preface

Entries within each section are listed alphabetically by author, apart from in the case of periodicals which are ordered according to the name of the publication. Items are annotated and provide a summary of the contents of each work, as well as other details, such as author, significance and viewpoint. An index of authors, titles and subjects is also included.

I would like to extend my appreciation to the many people who have helped me in this study. I would also like to thank the library staff at Pennsylvania State University's Berks and Schuylkill Campuses and Harrisburg Area Community College's Lebanon Campus for their assistance. My wonderful wife Connie and boys Ken and Andrew have been invaluable to me for their support and assistance.

Randall Fegley
Reading, Pennsylvania
March 1995

Introduction

In May 1993 Eritrea became Africa's newest independent nation. Named by the Italians in January 1890 after the Roman Erythraeum Mare (now the Red Sea), the country was an Italian colony from 1889 until the Second World War, when it came briefly under British mandate before being joined with Ethiopia as part of a federation in 1952. A decade later, Eritrea was formally annexed to Ethiopia and reduced to the status of a province. This led to a guerrilla insurgency that later crystallized into a national liberation movement. A three-decade war of independence, led by the Eritrean People's Liberation Front (EPLF), culminated in *de facto* independence for Eritrea in May 1991.

Shaped like an elongated triangle, Eritrea is situated on the African shore of the Red Sea, and has an area of 121,144 square kilometres (46,773 square miles), with a coastline extending for almost 1,000 kilometres (620 miles). The country is bounded to the north-west by Sudan, to the south and west by Ethiopia, and to the far south-east by Djibouti. Though a relatively small country by African standards, Eritrea has a varied topography and climate.

The Eritrean Plateau, which comprises the provinces of Hamassien, Serae, and Akele Guzai, covers nearly one-third of Eritrea's territory and is home to more than half of its population. Asmara, Eritrea's capital, is also located in this region at 2,325 metres (7,628 feet) above sea level. Averaging an altitude of around 1,980 metres (6,500 feet) above sea level, the plateau is broken in many places by the tributaries of the Tekeze, Mereb, and Gash rivers. Most of the usually moist highland areas have brownish to grey and black soils that contain some clay and are suitable for growing crops. Deforestation and centuries of continuous exploitation, however, have greatly reduced the productive capacity of these highland areas.

At the base of an escarpment leading down to the sea is Massawa, the main port, which is connected to the capital city by a railway and an all-weather road. The low and narrow coastal plain, which is below

499 metres (1,640 feet) in elevation, stretches for about 997 kilometres (620 miles) along the Red Sea and is mainly arid; it covers about one-fifth of Eritrea's territory but less than one-tenth of the population live there. Those that do are predominantly nomads. On the Red Sea coast, brown and red-brown soils are found in the foothills and on the slopes of the coastal mountains, and both sandy and saline soils prevail in the coastal strip. The very low annual rainfall in the area, however, makes these soils of negligible agricultural use. The country's territory also includes the Dahlak islands, a large, low-lying coral archipelago offshore near Massawa.

The western lowlands, which stretch along the Sudanese border, have elevations ranging between 1,600 feet (487 metres) and 6,500 feet (1,980 metres). These lowlands, which cover about two-fifths of the country's territory and are inhabited by about one-third of the population (mostly nomads and semi-nomads), are mainly flat and potentially fertile. The north-west semi-arid area of this region is enriched by the seasonally flowing Baraka River, which brings the benefits of rich soil and water for irrigation. The agriculturally productive lands of the Gash, Setit and Baraka river valleys have fertile black soils of alluvial and colluvial origin, which are constantly renewed and desalinated by high floodwaters.

Rainfall is less than 400 millimetres per year in the lowlands, increasing to 900 millimetres in parts of the highlands. The temperature gradient is similarly steep, with average annual temperatures ranging from a temperate 17°C (63°F) in the highlands to 30°C (86°F) in Massawa. The average temperature difference between winter and summer in the highlands is about 6.5°C (12°F). The coastal climate is very hot and dry with little or no fluctuations in daily, monthly, and seasonal temperatures. The Danakil depression in the south-east, which is more than 130 metres (426 feet) below sea level in places, experiences some of the highest temperatures recorded on earth, frequently exceeding 49°C (120°F). The western lowland region has varied climatic conditions: arid, semi-arid, and savanna. Annual rainfall ranges from 250 millimetres in the semi-arid areas to 500 millimetres in the savanna area, with arid areas receiving less than 200 millimetres of precipitation.

The Eritrean people

Eritrea's population in 1994 was estimated to be about 2.8 million, whilst other estimates claim up to 3.5 million inhabitants. Large returning refugee populations have made more accurate counting elusive. Although the bulk of the country's population live in rural areas, Eritrea is more urbanized than neighbouring Ethiopia and Sudan: about twenty-five to thirty per cent of Eritreans lived in cities and large towns in the early 1990s. Asmara (Asmera), the capital and largest city of Eritrea, is located at the northern end of the central Ethiopian plateau. Like Addis Ababa at the southern end, it has an altitude of about 2,285 metres (7,500 feet) and a temperate climate. Developed under Italian tutelage, it has the physical structure and amenities of an Italian town. With a population of around 500,000, the city is a centre of communications and trade, connected by railway to Massawa, Keren and Agordat. Asmara airport is one of the most modern in Africa. Eritrea's other major cities and towns are Keren, Massawa (Mitsiwa), Assab (Asseb/Aseb), Agordat, Adi Ugri, Dekamere (Dekemhare), Teseney, Barentu, and Nak'fa, which have a combined population of approximately 450,000.

The most important of these cities is the country's chief port, Massawa. The name 'Massawa' first applied to the outermost island of two. Now connected to the mainland by a rail causeway, its architecture displays its Turkish-Arab heritage, since it did not come under Ethiopian administration until after the Second World War, despite its significance as the gateway to and from Ethiopia for trade and communication. The small Eritrean navy is based in Massawa.

The port of Assab on the Red Sea, just north of the present-day border with Djibouti, was an ancient port of entry for seafarers and colonizers from South Arabia, but it was never able to compete with Djibouti or Massawa's facilities, and fell into disuse. In the late 1970s, however, Soviet aid to Ethiopia led to port development and the establishment of crude-oil bunkers. Since that time, a United States company has built a refinery there.

Eritrea is a multi-ethnic nation in which each ethnic group has its own language and cultural practices. In terms of religion, the population is fairly evenly divided between the Tigrinya-speaking Christians, the traditional inhabitants of the highlands, and various Muslim communities of the western lowlands, northern highlands and east coast, with a scattering of Catholics and traditional believers. The major languages of Eritrea are Tigrinya and Tigre, which are spoken by over three-quarters of the population. Tigrinya is spoken primarily by the inhabitants of the highlands, including the provinces of Hamassien, Serae, and Akele Guzai, and parts of the city of Keren. Tigre is spoken by most of the largely Muslim population of the north-eastern coastal plains and the western lowlands.

After the Amhara of Ethiopia, the Tigray constitute the second largest category of Ethio-Semitic speakers. The Ford Foundation's

1970 language survey numbered them at more than 3.5 million in both Eritrea and Ethiopia, although other estimates tend to be much lower. Their language, Tigrinya, is much closer to the ancient Ethiopian liturgical language, Ge'ez, than the Amharic of Ethiopia. Like the Amhara, the Tigray are chiefly plough agriculturists and Ethiopian Orthodox Christians. Despite some differences in dialect, the various Tigray clans feel that they have a common kinship with other Tigray regardless of their place of habitation. The number of persons speaking other Ethio-Semitic languages falls off sharply from the levels of the Amhara and the Tigray. Moreover, unlike them, members of these other groups do not share the Aksumite heritage and Orthodox Christianity, and their traditional economic base tends to be different.

The northern district of Hamassien, which, together with Seraye and Akele Guzai, makes up the central area of Eritrea, was part of the Aksumite Empire until the 8th century. An important Catholic mission existed there in 1869 and later an agricultural colony was set up at Shotil. A sizeable proportion of the populace is Muslim, although Christianity is the official religion. The strongest Eritrean opposition to control from Addis Ababa has historically been based in the Hamassien area. The region of Akele Guzai is specifically referred to in pre-Christian literature as one of three highland provinces of ancient Ethiopia. Close to Muslim areas and tribes of the Massawa region it was still loyal to Monophysite Christianity and its main language is Tigrinya. Originally Cushitic, its colonization by South Arabian traders and settlers led to an important infusion of Semitic culture and language. The area's influence, along with Aksum's, grew until the 7th century when the centre of power began to shift southward toward the Shewan region. Akele Guzai in more recent centuries was the subject of Catholic proselytization via the Portuguese, French and Italians.

Tigre, related to Tigrinya, was spoken by an estimated 117,000 persons in 1970, but that figure is likely to be an underestimate. The language is Semitic like Tigrinya, but has altered so drastically that speakers of one language cannot understand the other. Tigre was unwritten until Dawit Amanuel at the Swedish Mission translated the New Testament in 1890 and began a dictionary. The language now appears to be dying out because of the imposition of Tigrinya and because Arabic has become widely used in trading. The ten or so Eritrean groups or clusters of groups speaking the language do not constitute an ethnic entity, although they do share an adherence to Islam. The term 'Tigre' means 'serf' and is still used locally to refer to what has been called the serf class, as opposed to the aristocracy.

Originally the Tigre groups were Muslim vassals of the Bet Asgede, and although in the 19th century, these rulers adopted the language and religion of their subjects, they kept them as serfs. The Bet Asgede is made up of three autonomous groups, Habab, Ad Tekles and Ad Temaryam (Christian names revealing their former religion). They are primarily nomadic herdsmen, except for the Ad Tekles who have settled in the Keren district.

Probably the largest of the Tigre-speaking peoples are the Beni Amer, a mainly pastoral people living in the semi-arid region of the north and west, scattered on both sides of the border with Sudan. Originally they spoke a North Cushitic language. Except for the fact that the distinction between nobles and serfs seems to have been important, little is known of social and political organization among Tigre groups, except for the Beni Amer who were organized as a tribal federation with a paramount chief. The other Tigre groups are largely cultivators, and some, who live along the Red Sea coast and on the Dahlak islands, are active in fishing. These groups seem to have been autonomous units, but the effects of the Eritrean war for independence on the local political and social systems of the Tigre are not known.

Another Eritrean ethnic group is the Afar. Called the Danakil (in Arabic) or Adal by their neighbours, the Afar, a Muslim people of 'Hamitic' origin, were estimated to number no more than a total of 400,000 people north of the Djibouti-Addis Ababa railway in southern Eritrea, Ethiopia and Djibouti combined in 1970. Despite their relatively small numbers, they are of some importance because of their location between the highlands and the Red Sea, their antipathy to Ethiopian rule, and the quasi-autonomy of a section of Afar under the Sultan of Aussa before the revolution. There has also been more anthropological interest in the Afar than in any other ethnic group in the Horn of Africa. Except for several petty centralized states under sultans or sheikhs, the Afar are fragmented among tribes, sub-tribes, and still smaller clan divisions and are marked by a distinction between noble (red) and commoner (white) groups, about which little is known. Most Afar are pastoralists but are restricted in their nomadism by the need to stay close to permanent wells in extremely arid country. Some Afar in the former Sultan of Aussa's territory have long been settled cultivators in the lower Awash River Valley, and a programme to settle others along the middle Awash was initiated during the administration of the empire. Around 10,000 Afar live in the dry, barren region called the Danakil Depression, where they work the salt flats of Lake Karum, providing pure, white, ready-to-use salt for a large area of north-eastern Africa. The bars of this salt were once the currency of the Horn of Africa.

In the past the Afar were mainly dominated by the Tigray and Amhara. The latter had to conduct six campaigns, however, before they were able to subdue the Afar who still remember and resent their conquest by Ras Darge (Sahle Selassie). The Boran and Guji Afar both define their history as the 'good era' (before the Amhara) and the 'bad era' (after). During the Italian occupation the Afar regarded the Italians as less oppressive, perhaps because the occupiers permitted an 'open season' on the Amhara. In more recent years the Afar in the lower Awash valley were led by Sultan Ali Mira Hanfere until his self-exile in June 1975. They resisted the rural land reform programme of the Derg and after the sultan left, his people ransacked the unpopular Tendaho cotton and sugar plantation. Tendaho was a sore point with the Afar as the central government had expropriated some 52,000 hectares, thus depriving the Afar of a large section of grazing land.

The area between the Tigrinya and Tigre to the west and the Afar to the south-east is inhabited by the Saho. Saho is a linguistic category (based on a shared eastern Cushitic tongue) rather than a specific ethnic group. The origins of the diverse groups speaking this language are mixed, including elements from the Afar, Tigray, Tigre-speakers, and others, including some Arabs. Religiously, they are also varied. Most are Muslims but several groups, most notably the Erob in eastern Agame, are heavily influenced by the Tigray and are Ethiopian Orthodox Christians. The largest clan of the Saho is the Asawerta, numbering some 18,000, many of whom were probably nominally Christian under Zara Ya'qob (Zera Yaqoob) (1434-68) but are now Muslims of the Mirghaniya order, like the Beni Amer and Hahab. The next largest group are the Meni-Fere whose ancestry contains two interesting legends; one is that they derive from 'Mena' of royal Abyssinian stock, and the other (after they became Muslim) traces a connection to the Prophet Mohammed. Saho-speaking nomadic and semi-nomadic people occupy the eastern edge of the highlands and the foothills of the coastal plains. As pastoralists they are now quite peaceful, though in the 1860s they appeared in travellers' tales as wild and feared robbers. Clans elect their leaders democratically.

The sole Eritrean group speaking a Northern Cushitic tongue are the Beja, a Muslim pastoral group found in even larger numbers in neighbouring Sudan. Their language has been influenced by Arabic, and since their conversion to Islam they have come to claim Arab descent. Like many of the other nomadic pastoralists in the area, the

Beja are split into tribes and smaller units, based on descent from a common male ancestor and characterized by considerable autonomy. Nevertheless, these clans are federated under a paramount chief. The Beni Amer are a sub-group of the Beja who straddle the Eritrea-Sudan border with about 60,000 living in Eritrea and perhaps half that number in the Sudan. Despite their diverse Beja, Arab and Tigray origins, they began forming coherent chiefdoms in the 16th century and over the next century were incorporated into the Funj Confederation of Sennar. Their paramount chief received from the Funj a three-horned cap as the symbol of authority and this is still worn today. There is a general uniformity of law among them emphasizing distinctions between rulers and commoners. Some speak To-Bedawe and others Tigrinya. In the first half of the 19th century Mohammed Othman al-Mirghani and his sons preached among them and Islam with a strong Sufi flavour took hold. There are Mirghani centres at Kassala and Keren, while other Beni Amer revere the tomb of Sayyid Mustafa at Agordat. They engage in a seasonal migration to pick cotton in the Sudan.

Other ethnic groups include the Baria, Kunama, Nara, Bilayn, Hedareb and Rashaida. The Baria and Kunama are two negroid tribes that live in the Barentu area of Eritrea on the Sudanese border. The Baria inhabit the eastern Gash in the western lowlands and the Kunama and the related Nara live near the Setit and Gash rivers. The Kunama, also called 'Bazen' by the Amhara, and 'Baza' by the Sudanese, are more numerous (about 15,000) than the Baria (about 9,500). An 1861 estimate of 100,000 Kunama appears high, although there is no doubt that they were decimated in slave raids by both Egyptians and the Amhara. Both groups are sedentary agriculturalists living in villages, and both had matrilineal descent systems before the Baria were forcibly Islamized in about 1856. The traditional equality of women that had characterized the Baria was eliminated at that time. The term 'Baria' along with 'Shankalla' has also been used as a derogatory label for people with negroid characteristics. Unlike the Baria, the Kunama retained matrilinealism. Until Swedish missionaries realized they should concentrate their efforts on the women in the 1920s, the number of converts between 1866-70 was very few. The first books printed in the Kunama tongue were produced in 1903 by the Swedish mission. Today, about a third of the Kunama are Christian, either Roman Catholic or Protestant, but the Baria remain Muslim.

Both a region and an ethnic group, the Bilayn (or Bogos) is the most northerly district of Tigray, divided from that province by the Mereb River. Its 19th-century northern border with Egypt was so poorly defended by Tigray rulers that its people, the Bilayn, were prey to slave and cattle raiders from the Egyptian-dominated Sudan. Keren (also called Senhet), the principal centre of the Bilayn, was occupied by the Egyptian agent, Münzinger, in July 1872. The return of all of the Bilayn to the Ethiopian Empire was guaranteed by the Treaty of Adowa in 1884 but the Italians, despite promises to the contrary, annexed the area. This occupation was legalized in 1889 by the Treaty of Ucciali. Today the Bilayn people of the northern highlands are wedged between the Tigray and the Tigre-speakers. The people comprise two main clans: the Bet Teqwe and the Gebre Terqe. Each clan numbers about 15,000, representing, it is believed, two different waves of migration into the area from Lasta and Tigray by Agew peoples in the 13th or 14th century. Bilayn is spoken in Keren and the surrounding area. The Bilayn have a social system based on a hereditary chieftainship, and settled peasant farmers who may never rise to the status of the ruling class, though they own their land and have freedom of movement. Many Bilayn became Christians, though it was noted in the 1840s that they had neither priests nor churches. Nevertheless, they later took on the protective colouration of being Muslims in the mid-19th century in an attempt to save themselves from the depredations of the Egyptians and the Beni Amer. The Gebre Terqe were slower to become Islamized because of the assiduous efforts of Roman Catholic and Swedish Evangelical missionaries; a quarter of the population is still Catholic today. Other estimates suggest that about half of the Bilayn are Christians and the other half are Muslims.

The Hedareb, a nomadic group, live in the north-east and north-west border region; all are Muslim. The Rashaida, a nomadic people who migrated from the Arabian peninsula several hundred years ago are also found in small shifting concentrations in both Eritrea and the Sudan.

Many Eritreans speak more than one language; a large number of Muslims speak Arabic, and highland Eritreans speak Amharic. Some Italian and French is spoken by the older urbanites and English by middle-aged and younger people. English is rapidly becoming the language of business and is the medium of instruction at secondary schools and at university. Arabic is also widely spoken.

Ancient roots

Settled culture in Eritrea dates far back into the beginnings of history. In ancient times Eritrea saw the domestication and breeding of buffalo, savanna goats and woolly sheep. At some point before the birth of Christ, the dromedary was also brought to the arid lowlands of northern Eritrea. Like the Amhara to the south, the peoples of highland Eritrea grew a type of millet, teff (*Eragrostis abyssinica*), as their principal grain. This tiny-grained crop, which can grow at high altitudes and under quite dry conditions, is used to make *injera*, the pancake bread which is the staple food of the region. Along the coast, the trade in pearls has been historically important.

Eritrea has had a long historical association with Ethiopia (at times called Abyssinia). Immigrants from the Hadhramaut (southern Yemen) settled the region beginning about 1000 BC. These people were the founders of the Aksumite empire and controlled the northern Ethiopian Plateau between the 4th century BC and the 7th century AD. Established sometime before the 1st century AD, the empire of Aksum (Axum) encompassed Eritrea, northern Ethiopia and parts of present-day Sudan, Yemen and Saudi Arabia. Just south of the Eritrean border, the northern Ethiopian province of Tigray contains the holy city Aksum and the monasteries established by the 'nine saints'. The area is properly considered the birthplace of both Eritrea and Ethiopia. Like the Eritreans across the border, its people speak Tigrinya. Eritrea was a core area of the Aksumite Empire, as all trade and communications passed through the port of Adulis, near present-day Massawa. It was the gateway to the empire and its political orientation was crucial to the state. Rich in archaeological sites, the city of Aksum is revered by Eritrean and Ethiopian Christians alike. The Ark of the Covenant, the basis of Askum's status as Ethiopia's holiest place, is believed to have been brought here from Jerusalem in the 10th century BC and is said to rest in the church of St. Maryam Tseyon.

Aksumite connections with both Greek and Judaeo-Christian traditions are very strong. The word 'Ethiopia' is rooted in the 9th-century BC Greek of Homer and in the 5th century BC Herodotus' used the word 'aethiopes' to denote people with skins darker than Greeks (its literal meaning is 'burnt skin'). Coins, inscriptions, and tablets testify to 1st century AD contacts with Greeks, and in the 4th century, two Hellenized Syrian brothers introduced Christianity to the Aksumite court. The 4th-century King Ezana decreed Christianity as the state religion and built huge stone stelae with inscriptions giving the history of his reign; one of these stelae was taken to Rome by the Italians as booty from their 1935 invasion. Despite divergent positions taken at Chalcedon several hundred years later, there are some similarities between Greek and Ethiopian Orthodoxy. Before the spread of Islam which sealed the Horn of Africa off from Greek or other Mediterranean influence, the Greek language, its numerical system, and some law affected the mountain kingdom.

Monasteries and celibate teaching clergy were introduced into the Aksumite kingdom about 490 AD with the arrival of nine monks from various parts of the Roman Empire. They lived at court for twelve years, then spread out to found monasteries. Debra Damo is the region's oldest monastery. Founded in the 6th century, it is located on a rocky hill near Adigrat in Tigray just inside of Ethiopia. Accessible only to men, who pull themselves up by a rope hanging down, using foot holes cut into the rock, the site was chosen by Ze-Mikael Aregawi (one of the nine saints). Its church was probably not built until the 15th century. Its construction of alternating layers of stone and wood in rectangular form with the ceiling painted with floral designs, animals and crosses is considered one of the most beautiful in the Coptic tradition. Despite the ban on women, the Empress Seble Wengel, her daughters and their attendants took refuge there in 1541.

For seven centuries there is little information on monasticism in the region, then a notable expansion is documented in the 13th century with the activities of Iyasus Mo'a, Tekla Haymanot and Ewostatewos. By their own pious example they attracted disciples and championed higher moral standards, one going so far as to lecture an emperor on his attitudes toward marriage. The monasteries provided a pool of missionaries to go with the imperial army to Christianize newly-conquered areas.

The only qualification necessary to become a monk or a nun was a willingness to renounce all worldly pleasures and to devote one's life to prayer, fasting and humble chores. Monks did not even have to reside in a monastery; they could travel about or even stay in their own home. A monk had to attend a ceremony in which his body was declared dead and he was given a cloth skullcap, the symbol of his status. He was also freed of all debts, a possible motivation for some of these renunciations. However, anyone who took up the life of a monk must have the permission of his wife and if he did so to avoid his obligations to his family, he risked excommunication. Women were not encouraged to become nuns until they were aged fifty and widowed. Nonetheless, there were many in the history of the church who left their husbands and children to join a religious community or to form one. Convents usually grew up beside an important monastery. Many were established in the 13th century.

One of the most noteworthy rulers of Aksum was King Kaleb (Caleb) who reigned from around 514 to 543 AD. Known also as 'Elle-Atsbeha,' his existence is verified by Cosmas Indicopleustes, a 6th-century Greek merchant and writer, and Procopius, the historian who served Byzantine emperor Justinian. Kaleb responded to Justinian's request to wage war on Dhu Nuwas of Himyar (present-day Yemen) who had converted to Judaism and was persecuting Christians in retaliation for Justinian's persecution of Jews. Kaleb's expedition during 525 AD annihilated the Himyarite army. Gold, silver, and bronze coins have been found from his reign. Kaleb abdicated in favour of one of his four sons and took up the monastic life; his saint's day in the Ethiopian calendar is 20 Genbot (May 28).

Aksumite kings once occupied territory extending from Yemen across the Red Sea to Meröe along the Nile in the Sudan north of Khartoum. Aksum declined by the 7th century when the Persians ended Christian rule in South Arabia and cut off trade. A king named Armah, possibly an apocryphal figure, is believed to have been the king of Aksum at that time. He is said to have befriended disciples of the Prophet Mohammed who had fled persecution in Arabia. Some scholars believe that without Armah's support and assistance, Islam might not have survived. The only positive response to Mohammed's proclamation urging the world's rulers to 'worship the One God' came from the Christian monarch Armah. As a result, it is believed that Mohammed issued a prohibition against any offensive moves against Ethiopia, an edict respected until the 16th century. During Armah's reign, Aksumite influence in South Arabia ended, but he continued to control the Red Sea area and favoured good relations with the Arabs because of mutual trade. He also continued the policy of allowing Muslim refugees to come to Ethiopia. When Mohammed asked him to permit these exiles to return, Armah agreed and the emigrés were sent to Medina where Mohammed had fled to escape his antagonists in Mecca.

Located just south of present-day Massawa, the ancient port of Adulis was one of the most important Aksumite settlements in Eritrea. A traveller in the 1st century AD described the town as a 'fair-sized village'. Written between 277 and 290 AD an inscription on a building in the old port described the campaigns of an early Aksumite king into south Arabia and the Beja lands of the eastern Sudan. In 525 AD Cosmos Indicopleustes noted Adulis as a flourishing port trading with Arabia, Persia and India.

To protect their Red Sea commerce, Arab Muslims occupied the Dahlak Archipelago off Massawa in the 7th century; inscriptions on tombstones (now taken to museums in Treviso, Modena, and Cairo) provide the names of the reigning families in the 12th and 13th centuries, who engaged in commerce. Great cisterns for water storage have been found, as these islands, along with Massawa, have one of the hottest climates in the world. Its present-day inhabitants are mainly Tigre-speaking, and their only resource is fishing for pearls and mother-of-pearl, and breeding sparse herds of goats and camels.

After the expansion of the Aksumite empire into the south in the 9th century, emperors lived in Lasta, Amhara and Shewa. By AD 950 much of highland Eritrea was part of the Abyssinian empire, its principal port of foreign trade being Massawa, which was largely autonomous. The separatist tendencies of Tigray and Eritrea were already apparent in the 13th century and Amde Tseyon (1314-44) was obliged to re-conquer the area and post a military colony there. Aksum remained the cultural centre of the church and in 1434 Emperor Zara Ya'qob undertook the long journey from Shewa to Aksum to be invested with his crown. The expansion of Christianity in Shewa and Gojam was the work of priests trained in Tigray monasteries. Rulers of Tigray were known as the Bahr-negash ('King of the Sea') though they had little actual authority over the 'sea' after the Ottoman empire occupied Massawa in 1557.

During the Middle Ages and the early modern era, the Eritrean coast was a prominent trading area. It was the terminus of the Gondar-Massawa trade route and the port for numerous sea lanes throughout the Red Sea. Its markets and warehouses dealt in pearls, leather, coffee and qat. Qat or Khat (Catha edulis or celastrua edulis) is a plant with mild narcotic properties. Its only identifiable pharmacological component is non-methylated epherdrine, a derivative of which is used for the relief of asthma and some allergies. When chewed it produces a pleasant insomnia in small doses and slight intoxication in larger amounts. Used for centuries, Muslim men and only women said to possess occult powers are permitted to chew it. An early account reported that it kept scholars from falling asleep over their books. Workers may chew it in the early morning and then work until evening without stopping. Qat plays a great part in Muslim social life; great chewings take place at festivals of birth, circumcision, marriage and tomb vigils. Amde Tseyon's chronicler in the early 13th century wrote that his Muslim enemies intended to plant qat in the lands of the Christians when he defeated them. Ethiopia is the main commercial producer of qat, exporting the leaves through Eritrea to South Arabian customers.

Muslims and Europeans

Throughout the 1500s, Eritrea and the Christian Empire of Ethiopia came under increasing threat from Muslim forces, both local and foreign. Under the command of Ahmed ibn-Ibrahim al-Ghazi, a Muslim force from Harar defeated the small Ethiopian force that had come to collect the tribute refused by the king of Adal in 1527. Two years later Ahmed's army won a decisive victory over the Christians at Shembera Kure. They went on to occupy Dewaro and Shewa in 1531, Amhara and Lasta in 1533, and invaded Tigray in 1535. Emperor Lebna Dengel became a fugitive with two-thirds of his empire under occupation and the royal women hidden in safety in the Debra Damo monastery.

On Lebna Dengel's death in 1540 his son, Gelawdewos, inherited a small, demoralized and desertion-prone army. However, in February 1541, he was given new hope by the news that Portuguese ships were anchored at Massawa. An appeal for military aid was answered by 400 Portuguese volunteers under the command of Christavão da Gama. Joined to the army of Tigray, they defeated the Muslim army of occupation early in 1542. Ahmed retreated, but was aided by the Turkish Pasha of Zebid in the form of 900 Arab, Turkish and Albanian mercenaries, who helped win the next encounter. There were heavy casualties, including half of the Portuguese contingent, and da Gama was captured and beheaded. Ahmed confidently dismissed his mercenaries. In October 1542 Emperor Gelawdewos, who had been in Shewa during the first two battles, linked his army with the northern group in Semen. They took the offensive and won a decisive victory near Lake Tana on 21 February 1543. Ahmed was killed, and his army dispersed in disorder. His wife married her husband's nephew, Nur, after he promised to renew the conquest of Ethiopia. Campaigns were mounted from 1545 to 1559, ending when Nur's army killed Gelawdewos who had unwisely put his troops into battle at the end of a fasting period and had ordered them to attack before they were in a position to surround the Muslims. Harar's military capability was finally extinguished in 1577 by Emperor Sarsa Dengel (Sartsa Dengel) with Portuguese help.

Undoubtedly, the Portuguese saved the Abyssinian Empire from being swallowed up by its Muslim invaders. However, over the next half century the Portuguese would wear out their welcome as Jesuit missionaries sought to convert the Empire from its ancient Coptic traditions to Roman Catholicism. They would be expelled in 1634.

In the north, the Ottoman Turks had taken control of Massawa and Arkiko in Eritrea and Suakin in the Sudan in 1557. Their plan was to take the large area extending from Suakin to Massawa which they called Habesh (or Habash). Their soldiers had moved into Agame where they profaned churches. The Tigrayans moved north to counter the threat and the Turks were forced to fall back and confine themselves to the Red Sea ports. In 1578 Sarsa Dengel defeated the invaders, but a peace agreement with the Turks was not obtained until

1589. That same year, after numerous rebuffs by the forces of both the Bahr-negash and the Ethiopian emperor, the Turks handed over control to a chieftain of the Belew who was titled *na'ib* (deputy). For some two and a half centuries during successive periods of Turkish and Egyptian control, the *na'ibs* were notorious for their onerous taxes on trade and their harassment of both Christian pilgrims going to Jerusalem and Muslims going to Mecca.

Relations between the coastal rulers and the Ethiopian emperor were deadlocked for years. Eventually the *na'ibs* were unable to maintain their exorbitant taxes on transit trade because they depended on provisions from the interior and because they feared armed intervention. Nevertheless the Ethiopian emperors could not exert effective control over the coast because both Massawa and Arkiko were protected by cannon and could not be captured.

In the diaspora after Constantinople fell to the Turks in 1463, a number of Greeks made their way to Ethiopia; several held positions of honour at the courts of Iyasu I (1602-1706), Bekaffa (1721-30) and Iyasu II (1730-55). Both Empress Mentewab and her son Iyasu II studied Greek and letters were written in that language to the Greek Patriarch of Alexandria (though the Coptic Patriarch named Ethiopia's bishops) inviting priests, carpenters, and goldsmiths, and asking for holy books. A Greek clerical mission arrived in 1755, but Iyasu died soon after and conditions were too unsettled for any ecumenical discussions.

The title of Bahr-negash was changed to Ras by the time of Mikael Sehul (c. 1740-80) who was on good enough terms with the *na'ibs* to acquire muskets which enabled him to extend his power inland to Gondar. His descendants, Welde Selassie (1780-1816) and Sebagades (1822-31), ruled until Webe Haile Mariam gained control from 1831 to 1855 and in the 19th century Egypt began a general expansion southward into the Sudan and adjacent areas. In 1846 Massawa was transferred to Egyptian control. This angered Webe, who launched a series of raids against the coast. He failed to capture Massawa and Ottoman rule was resumed for a short time. All of these Tigrayan rulers considered themselves the true defenders of the Coptic faith and the Solomonic dynasty until Kasa Haylu (Tewodros II) defeated Webe in 1855. Massawa was again ceded to Egypt in 1866. The Egyptians then invaded the highlands, seizing Keren and Asmara.

Around this time, British influence in the region began to grow in significance. British connections with Eritrea date from the 1700s and early 1800s when numerous travellers and several military and diplomatic missions passed through the country on the way to or from Ethiopia and the upper reaches of the Nile. Samuel Johnson's writing on Abyssinia in the 1730s and the publication in 1790 of the adventures of James Bruce led to increased British interest in Eritrea and Ethiopia. Then, throughout 1804 and 1805 and again in 1810, Viscount Valentia sent Henry Salt from Massawa to the highlands. He was followed by Nathaniel Pearce, who spent twelve years in Tigray, where William Coffin also resided from 1810 until his death.

From 1841 to 1843 Cornwallis Harris led an Anglo-Indian mission to Shewa and signed a poorly understood, and therefore moot, treaty of commerce with Emperor Sahle Selassie. An adventurer, John Bell, served Ras Ali Alula and then Emperor Tewodros from 1841 until his death in 1860; Mansfield Parkyns resided in Tigray from 1843-46, marrying an Ethiopian woman and adopting the country's life style and customs. Walter Plowden, Bell's travelling companion in 1844, was named the first British consul at Massawa in 1847. By the time of Plowden's death at the hands of a rival of Emperor Tewodros in 1860, British-sponsored Protestant missionary-artisans, many of German-Swiss extraction, were living under the patronage of the emperor.

Emperor Tewodros II was unable to gain the loyalty of all of Tigray. But in 1861, he did succeed in putting down the pretensions of Negus Welde Mikael, the protector of the Catholic missionaries, who aimed to get French help to establish a Catholic state in Tigray. Tewodros appointed Kasa and Gugsa Mercha of Temben to govern the region in 1864. After much internal warfare, Kasa Mercha declared himself ruler of all Tigray in 1867. He controlled enough to secure the march of the Anglo-Indian army through Tigray to Magdala to defeat Tewodros in 1868. Near the capital of Tigray, Adowa, was the battle in July 1871 that brought Kasa Mercha to the throne as Yohannes IV and relative stability to Tigray, except for attacks from Egypt in 1875 and 1876.

While all of this was unfolding another conflict dominated an important part of Eritrea. In the 1820s two clans, the Mensa and the Marya, living in close proximity to each other at Hazega and Tsazega in Hamassien, vied for power. This rivalry continued through the reigns of Tewodros and Yohannes IV until 1890 when Italy, in defiance of the limits set by the Treaty of Ucciali, occupied the area.

A Swiss scholar and businessman named Werner von Münzinger became deeply involved in Eritrean affairs around that time. He had settled in Keren in 1855, married a woman of the area, and studied the language, and the social, economic and legal life of the Bilayn people. Appointed vice-consul at Massawa by the British in 1863, he also served France in the same capacity, becoming an ardent protector of the Catholic missions in the region and working to separate the province from Ethiopia. In 1868 he took an active part in preparations for the British expedition against Tewodros. In 1865 the lease on Suakin and Massawa, which had lapsed after the death of Egypt's leader, Muhammad Ali, was renewed in favour of Khedive Ismail; he appointed Münzinger as governor of Massawa in 1871. Münzinger was later made commander of the Egyptian troops stationed in the eastern Sudan. Meanwhile the conflict between Egypt and Ethiopia intensified.

Some 2,500 Egyptian troops landed at Massawa and Senhet (Keren) between August and October 1875. They proceeded inland to the border of Tigray and Yohannes IV declared war on October 23. Dispatched by the Khedive Ismail on a mission to seek the co-operation of Menelik of Shewa against Ethiopian Emperor Yohannes IV, Münzinger, his wife, Menelik's envoy to the Khedive and a party of Sudanese soldiers were killed by the Afar on 13 November 1875. The next day Tigrayan general Ras Alula engaged some Egyptian troops at Gundet. His full force (an estimated 60,000 men) surrounded the Egyptians the night of the 15th and defeated them in a one-hour battle. Yohannes captured the Remington rifles used by the Egyptians, eighteen artillery pieces, ammunition, supplies and 20,000 thalers. Keeping the defeat at Gundet secret, the Khedive formed a new expeditionary force on 26 November 1875. An estimated 12,000 troops debarked at Massawa on 11 January 1876. Two-thirds of the force advanced to Gura and one-third to Kayakhor by the first week in February. Yohannes moved out with a large force (estimates vary from 45,000-200,000) from Adowa on 3 February. Three weeks later they were within striking distance of Gura. Ras Alula commanded the advance guard which attacked near Kayakhor on 7 March. They pursued the retreating Egyptians to Gura a few miles away. Through the 8th and 9th of March, the Ethiopians besieged the Egyptian-held fort at Gura and despite heavy losses from the fort's artillery, managed to capture thousands of rifles and some fifteen cannon. The Egyptians sued for peace.

By October 1883, Ras Alula felt confident enough to renew the offensive. This time he moved on Ailet (Aylet), on the coastal plain near Massawa, which is the site of hot springs that serve as a spa for people seeking cures for syphilis, rheumatism, fevers and dysentery. It had been a point of contention between Egypt and Ethiopia since the 1860s. Forced to curtail their empire, a bankrupt Egypt withdrew from Massawa in 1885. Ras Alula ended the Egyptian threat, but did not occupy Massawa. Before the Ethiopians could grasp control of coastal Eritrea, a greater challenge emerged in the form of the Italians, who as latecomers to colonialism felt the need to catch up with the other European powers quickly. The end result of this would be the splitting of the old province of Tigray into Ethiopian Tigray and Italian Eritrea.

One other group of Europeans which deserves a mention as a significant source of influence on Eritrea and the surrounding region in the late 1800s is the Greeks. Even after Greece became a nation again in 1830, Greeks continued to come to Eritrea and Ethiopia as skilled craftsmen, merchants, farmers and builders. Many married Ethiopian women, and though they tended to form separate communities, they integrated well into Ethiopian life. Since Greece was a weak nation, the Ethiopians did not perceive them as the advance guard of an invasion to the Ethiopians. Despite their manifest contributions, Greeks were looked down on by other Europeans as inferior and not worthy of being counted as 'Europeans'; thus they were ignored socially along with Armenians, Indians, Arabs and Ethiopians. The first official Greek envoy to Ethiopia was Demosthenes Mitzakis, sent in 1879. His government was particularly interested in economic ties between Greece and Ethiopia, via Eritrea. Mitzakis did much to soothe Ethiopian-British relations. As a result of Mitzakis' friendship with Yohannes IV, a Greek physician named Nicolas Parisis, was sent to attend the emperor from February 1885 to June 1886. Parisis was a thorn in the side of the Italians who at that time were busy trying to justify their occupation of Massawa. Parisis was just one of many and the names of Greeks who served the Ethiopian crown would make a long list.

Italian rule

Early contacts between the Horn of Africa and Italy were made in the 15th century when artisans from the city-states of Florence and Venice went to Ethiopia where they were employed by the emperors. In turn, Ethiopian priests went to Rome and attended the Council of Florence in 1441. A steady trickle of pilgrims led to the founding of the Vatican's Collegio Etiopico in 1539.

Italians were among both the Lazarist and the Capuchin missionaries who established stations on the Eritrean coast in 1838 and 1846 respectively. However, significant Italian interest in the south-western Red Sea coast only began in 1869 after the opening of the Suez Canal. Seeing the need for a refuelling station, one of the Lazarists, Giuseppe Sapeto, purchased the port of Assab from local sultans on behalf of the Rubattino Navigation Society. On the other hand, the Capuchins under the leadership of a Father Massaia, who resented the House of Savoy's curtailment of papal power, tended to oppose Italian designs on the area.

More than seventy Italian expeditions, backed by commercial and geographical societies, went to Africa in the last half of the 19th century. One of the more important ones politically was an 1876 mission to Shewa headed by the Marchese Orazio Antinori. The Italian Geographical Expedition was particularly willing to become an extension of government interest. A Milanese trade mission headed by Dr P. Matteuci visited Yohannes IV in 1879, but Yohannes was only interested in what the Italians could do to free his port of entry, Massawa, from Egyptian-British interference with his arms shipments. From that point on the Italian Foreign Office concentrated its efforts on Menelik of Shewa through an envoy, Count Pietro Antonelli. Following an agreement with the Sultan of Awsa, Antonelli pioneered the trade route from Assab to Shewa and on 21 May 1883, concluded a trade and friendship treaty with Menelik. Feeding Menelik's appetite for arms and his rivalry with Yohannes, the Italians signed a second agreement on 20 October 1887.

Meanwhile, Assab and its surrounding hinterland had been formally transferred to the Italian government in 1882. Two years later the rise of the Mahdi in the Sudan obliged the Egyptians to withdraw from East Africa. To facilitate their evacuation, the British signed a treaty with Emperor Yohannes in July 1884 promising him 'free transit' through Massawa in return for his co-operation. However, fearing expanding French influence, the British encouraged the Italian presence in the area. The Italians seized Massawa in February 1885, and in 1886 they pushed inland.

Ras Alula ordered the Italians to evacuate their garrisons at Wiha, Se'ati and Zula. On 25 January 1887, when he learned that a 550-man relief column was approaching to re-supply the garrisons, he immediately engaged some 7,500 troops against the Italians, virtually annihilating them. Yohannes was shocked, fearing that instead of deterring further Italian expansion into Ethiopia, Alula had provoked an all-out war and rebuked him though privately Ethiopian pride was boosted by the victory. Known to the Italians as the 'Dogali massacre,' the encounter, an unexpected victory by the forces of Ras Alula, is know as the Battle of Tedale to the Eritreans and Ethiopians.

By 1888 Yohannes saw the likelihood of escalating conflict with Italy. But threatened with action by both Menelik to the south and a Mahdist army massing on his border with the Sudan, he offered reconciliation and withdrew to fight the Mahdists at Gallabat where he lost his life. The Italians took advantage of the confusion following the death of the emperor to advance into the highlands.

Yohannes' successor was his old rival Menelik of Shewa. Crowned as Emperor Menelik II, he recognized the Italian occupation, signing the Treaty of Ucciali with the Italians on 2 May 1889. Negotiated by Antonelli, the treaty gave the Italian Government control over the colony, and the borders agreed upon in Article III of this treaty are now the borders of modern-day Eritrea. An Ethiopian delegation went to Rome to witness the ratification and to purchase armaments with the four million lira credit granted by the Italian parliament. However, Article XVII of the treaty, which the Ethiopians and many others interpreted to be a statement of co-operation and mutual defence, would be used by the Italian government to claim a protectorate over Ethiopia. On 1 January 1890, the king of Italy proclaimed the creation of the colony of Eritrea, named after the Mare Erythraeum (Red Sea) of the Roman geographers. Asmara was made the capital of the new colony. However, the Italians exceeded the agreed borders of the colony and Menelik, who refused to be an Italian puppet, declared war. Subsequently, Eritrea served as a base for an Italian invasion of Tigray in northern Ethiopia. In 1896 Menelik crushed the Italian armies at the battle of Adowa (Adwa), one of the most humiliating defeats suffered by a European colonial power in Africa. Despite its failure to penetrate Tigray, Italy retained control over Eritrea and established a diplomatic mission in Addis Ababa in 1897 and commercial agencies in various locations later on.

Following their defeat at Adowa the Italian public lost interest in their colony, although the Italian government and certain Italian companies did not neglect Eritrea. Italian farmers were encouraged to settle in areas declared Italian Crown Lands by the colonial government, covering, in particular, the fertile highland area. Under a succession of Italian governors beginning with Ferdinando Martini from 1898 to 1906 (followed by Salvago-Raggi, De Martino, Cerrina-Ferroni, Gasparini, Zoli Astuto dei Lucchesi, and Daodiace), the colony saw the development of a degree of unity and public order unique in a region marked by substantial cultural, linguistic and religious diversity. Eritrea experienced material progress in many areas before Ethiopia did so. Public-administered medical services, agricultural improvements, Italian-flavoured public amenities, banks, good roads and a railway were established.

The most important development during the period after 1890 was the growth of an Eritrean public administration. Local governments in the colony provided new district administrations to serve as links between the population and the central administration, particularly in the highlands. In other areas respect was paid to the indigenous political organization. Members of the indigenous Eritrean population were employed in the public service, particularly the police and public works, and their loyalty to the colonial rulers was fostered by granting them substantial emoluments and status symbols. The local population shared in the benefits conferred under Italian colonial administration.

Connections between Eritrea and the outside world were maintained by a number of shipping lines which stopped at Massawa. By the 1930s an Italian airline, Ala Littoria, had established a route from Rome to Massawa, via Benghazi, Cairo and Khartoum and continuing on to Djibouti, Addis Ababa and Mogadishu. In August 1928 the Ethiopian regent, Ras Tafari Mekonnen (who later became Emperor Haile Selassie) signed a twenty-year Friendship treaty with Italy which provided for a free-trade zone at Assab and joint construction of a road from Assab to Desse.

After Benito Mussolini assumed power in Italy, the spirit of the colonial government in Eritrea changed. With the Fascists in power in Italy, previously relaxed racial attitudes changed for the worse. The new administration emphasized the racial and political superiority of the Italians; segregation became the rule and local people were relegated to the lowest levels of public employment. Stricter racial laws were introduced and the education of Eritreans was curtailed.

State control in the political sphere was matched by greater control in the economic sphere. Agricultural improvements were carried out by quasi-governmental agencies which controlled particular sectors of the economy and developed a base for commercial agricultural products on farms run by Italians. Attempts at improving the efficient management of the colony, however, did not transform it into a self-sufficient entity. When Mussolini decided to invade Ethiopia, economic policy changed and after 1933 economic development programmes were inaugurated as part of war preparations, with special stress on improving the Massawa harbour and on enlarging the road network. With the arrival of large numbers of Italian invasion troops, Asmara and other towns underwent considerable expansion. The colony's most important function was to serve as a strategic base for Italian interests.

It was from her colonies of Eritrea and Somalia that Italy launched her conquest and occupation of Ethiopia in 1935. This attempt to avenge the humiliation of Adowa was brutally successful until British and Ethiopian forces recaptured the country in 1941. In December 1934 a small border clash known as the Wel Wel incident was the pretext used by Mussolini to 'justify' moving into Ethiopia, although the actual invasion did not occur until October 1935 because of the need to mass troops and supplies in Eritrea. On 5 October, Adowa and Adigrat capitulated without firing a shot after the Italians moved across the Mereb River, the border between Eritrea and Ethiopia.

Mekele, the capital of Tigray, fell a month later, again with little opposition.

Mussolini pressed his commander, Marshal de Bono, to drive southward. De Bono, claiming he needed time to resupply his forces for impending attacks in the mountainous Temben province, delayed movement so long that Mussolini replaced him with Marshal Badoglio in late November. The Ethiopians retreated, leading the Italians to extend their lines precariously since Badoglio was eager for victories. The Ethiopians, despite their lack of heavy weapons, struck back in late December in a 'Christmas offensive' and the Italians were routed by Ras Emru's column at the Dembequena Pass. At the same time, forces under Ras Kasa and Ras Seyum linked up in Temben and Ras Mulugeta pushed back toward Mekele. Badoglio sent urgent pleas for reinforcements and Mussolini promptly dispatched three more divisions. In a panic at the losses suffered at the hands of the Ethiopians, and with Mussolini's approval, Badoglio began to bomb military and civilian areas indiscriminately and to drop canisters of poison gas of various kinds, in violation of Italy's signing of the Geneva Convention of 1926. This illegal but effective warfare characterized the conflict.

In spite of these technological advantages, the Italians still found subduing Ethiopia to be a struggle. The Ethiopians almost wiped out the Italian garrison at Waryau. Moreover, it was only a lack of communications that prevented the Ethiopians from bringing all their forces to bear in this and other confrontations. The situation for the Italians was serious enough for Mussolini to initiate secret peace talks for a possible compromise peace. In the meantime, General Rodolfo Graziani, based in Italian Somaliland, launched an attack toward Negelle in the south-east. In the north, Badoglio began to move toward the mountainous stronghold of Amba Aradom with over 70,000 men and after three days of relentless bombing and artillery barrages, severely damaged the Ethiopian forces. The clash, known as the battle of Enderta, was over on 19 February 1936.

At the head of the largest European army ever engaged in a colonial war, Badoglio pushed north-west for the second battle of Temben. With 200,000 men under his command against 60,000 Ethiopians, Badoglio expected a quick victory, but frenzied waves of attacking Ethiopians almost routed the Third Italian Army and Eritrean Corps. The use of air power again proved decisive and the fleeing Ethiopian army was virtually destroyed; the battle was over on 29 February. Badoglio conquered the north and pushed towards Addis Ababa for a final victory. With the exception of units under the personal command of Emperor Haile Selassie he met little opposition to his march on

Gondar and other towns on the way to the capital. Aided by Oromo tribesmen, the Italians drove the emperor's forces towards Lake Ashenge where they carried out another aerial massacre. By the time Haile Selassie and the remnants of his army reached Addis Ababa, near the end of April, the capital was in panic. At the urging of his court, the monarch departed for Djibouti by rail on 5 May before Badoglio entered the city in triumph at the head of mechanized columns, while Graziani moved in westward through the Ogaden against little opposition.

When the Italians finally conquered Ethiopia they joined the country administratively to Somalia and Eritrea under the name 'Italian East African Empire.' In 1937 Italian King Victor Emmanuel III was proclaimed 'Emperor of Ethiopia', but a guerrilla war of resistance began shortly afterwards and the Italians were never able to fully bring the Ethiopians under their control.

Diplomatic relations between Ethiopia and Italy were resumed in 1948. A considerable amount of Italian influence is still apparent in the urban centres of both Eritrea and Ethiopia and Italian food, fashions and products continue to be highly regarded. Indeed, Asmara is almost a mirror image of an Italian city. Thousands of Italian farmers, technicians and businessmen flourished in Ethiopia and Eritrea until recently, while the country with the largest number of expatriate Ethiopians is Italy. Scholarship by Guidi, Cerulli, Zaghi, Conti Rossini, Ricci and many others, as well as the memoirs of hundreds of Italians who lived, fought, doctored, explored, and worked in Ethiopia, have made a knowledge of the Italian language necessary for scholars of Eritrean and Ethiopian studies.

British administration and the United Nations solution

In January 1941, early on in the Second World War, the British, anxious to secure their Red Sea supply route, attacked Eritrea from the Sudan. By April 1941 they had captured Asmara and established a military administration there. On 5 May 1941, British Commonwealth forces, under Brigadier Sanford and Colonel Orde Wingate, also liberated Ethiopia. The Emperor finally returned from exile, symbolically leading the troops into Addis Ababa.

Early relations between the British and powers in the Horn of Africa were uneasy, due partly to Britain's intervention in the area in 1868. In 1872 the Ethiopian Emperor sent an envoy to Europe to protest against Egyptian aggression to his borders, with the result that Henry King was appointed as his honorary consul in London. Nevertheless, Egypt attacked Ethiopia and though they were repulsed in 1875 and 1876, the peace process took ten more years. British General Charles 'Chinese' Gordon was employed by the Khedive to negotiate in 1877 and 1879. Only in 1884, needing Ethiopian co-operation against the Mahdists, did the British government send Vice Admiral Sir William Hewett to offer a treaty to Yohannes IV. An agreement was reached but as far as the Ethiopians were concerned, it was violated within the year, when the British government chose to do nothing to stop Italian encroachment. Britain abdicated its responsibility for enforcing the treaty to Italy, when that nation occupied Massawa in 1885. Missions headed by James Harrison-Smith in 1886 and by Gerald Portal in 1887 failed to reconcile Ethiopian resentment of Italy. Italy's defeat in 1896 led to increased British concern. Relations were again strained in 1906 when Britain, France and Italy made an agreement over their respective spheres of influence should the Ethiopian empire crumble in the event of Menelik's demise; the monarch was reassured only by strong guarantees of Ethiopia's independence. Borders with the Sudan, Egypt and British Somaliland were established by treaties between 1897 and 1906.

Relations between Britain and Eritrea and Ethiopia were interrupted during the Italian occupation which Britain recognized. London also gave refuge to Haile Selassie. After the war, Britain provided advisers to the Ethiopian Emperor in the fields of finance, education, economic development and defence, though the number gradually diminished as a result of both economic troubles in Britain and Haile Selassie's policy of diversifying foreign aid. Like the Italians, a number of Britons also developed strong interests in Eritrea and the Horn of Africa. Among the many British scholars in history, linguistics and other subjects related to Eritrea and Ethiopia are C. F. Beckingham, Edward Ullendorff, Richard Pankhurst, Spencer Trimingham and Richard Greenfield.

After the defeat of the Italians in 1941, Eritrea was governed by Britain (under administrators Stephen Longrigg and J. M. Benoy) until it was transferred to Ethiopia in 1952 by a United Nations General Assembly resolution. The Eritrean national identity, which was established during the Italian colonial period, was further subjugated under British rule. Moreover, in the midst of wartime and post-war economic constraints, the British administration did little to combat the neglect and decline of Eritrean industry and the continued exploitation of Eritrea's agricultural resources by Italian settlers.

A number of countries displayed an active interest in the area. In the immediate post-war years Italy requested that Eritrea be returned as a colony or as a trusteeship and this claim was initially supported by the Soviet Union, which anticipated a communist victory in the first post-war Italian elections. Yet, in 1947, as part of the peace terms drawn up to end the war, Italy agreed to renounce sovereignty over its colonies. The Arab states, seeing Eritrea and its Muslim population as an extension of the Arab world, then sought the establishment of an independent state. Some British favoured dividing the territory, with the idea that the Christian Tigrinya-speaking areas and the coast from Massawa southward would go to Ethiopia, and the largely Muslim north and north-west would go to Sudan.

The importance of the ports of Massawa and Assab cannot be over-estimated in analysing the difficulties which were to follow. Along with Djibouti, they are Ethiopia's only practical points of access to the sea and their necessity to Ethiopia was a vital element in the continuing battle over Eritrean secession. Ethiopia claimed that Eritrea must be reunited with its 'Ethiopian motherland', a claim which was supported by the Eritrean Unionist Party. Other parties, however, advocated either the resumption of Italian rule or independence. As the Allied powers and the newly-formed United Nations discussed the future of the former Italian colony, Ethiopian territorial claims helped to foment a more militant nationalism among the Eritrean population.

The Four Power Inquiry Commission established by the Allies (France, Britain, the Soviet Union, and the United States), failed to agree in their September 1948 report on a future course for the colony. Great Britain subsequently turned the problem over to the United Nations.

A United Nations commission, which arrived in Eritrea in February 1950, eventually approved a plan recommending some form of association with Ethiopia. In due course on 2 December 1950 the General Assembly adopted a resolution to that effect, with the provision that Britain, the administering power, should facilitate the UN efforts and depart from the colony no later than 15 September 1952. The UN General Assembly resolution, adopted by a vote of forty-seven to ten, provided that Eritrea should be linked to the Ethiopian empire through a loose federal structure under the sovereignty of the Ethiopian emperor but with a form of internal self-government. The federal government, in the same way as the existing imperial government, was to control foreign and defence affairs, foreign and inter-state commerce, transport, and finance. Control over domestic affairs (including police, local administration, and local taxation to meet its own budget) was to be exercised by an elected Eritrean assembly on the parliamentary model. The Eritrean state was to have its own administrative and judicial structures and a flag.

The above agreements were reached partly as a result of the strategic interests and diplomatic influence of the United States, who strongly supported the idea that a federation should be formed between Eritrea and Ethiopia. Faced with this constraint the British administration held elections on 26 March 1952 for a Representative Assembly of sixty-eight members. This body, made up of equal numbers of Christians and Muslims, accepted the draft constitution advanced by the UN commissioner on 10 July 1952. The constitution was ratified by the Ethiopian Emperor Haile Selassie on 11 September 1952, and the Representative Assembly was transformed into the Eritrean National Assembly three days before the federation was proclaimed.

Eritrean federation with Ethiopia was the result of a lengthy effort by Haile Selassie. Shortly after his restoration in 1941 the emperor sponsored an irredentist movement, which called for the incorporation of Eritrea and Italian Somaliland into Ethiopia. Within Eritrea itself, a local organization supported the movement and in 1944 became the Unionist Party, which enjoyed significant financial assistance from Ethiopia. Its members generally felt that Eritrea should be turned over to the Ethiopians at once and argued that it was a part of Ethiopia based on historical, cultural, geographical, religious, and economic association, and that it had been stolen by Italy. Although the unionist position was supported by a number of intellectuals, by 1946 it was being challenged by the newly-formed Muslim League led by Othman Salih Sabbe. Another anti-union splinter group, the National Muslim Party of Massawa was organized in 1947. A third predominantly Muslim group, the New Eritrean Pro-Italy Party, which enjoyed the support of local Italians and people of mixed (Afro-Italian) origin, was organized in late 1947. In addition, the New Eritrean Liberal Progressive Party, a predominantly Christian organization motivated by an antipathy toward Shewan (Amharic) domination, was also established in early 1947. Pro- and anti-unionist activity was encouraged in a legal and constitutional framework, first in conjunction with testimony before the United Nations commission of inquiry and, later, in preparation for the election of the Representative Assembly.

However, after October 1949 there was a steady rise in the level of violence and intimidation. Shortly after the arrival of the United Nations commission in February 1950, several of the anti-unionist parties began to splinter under pressure from the pro-Ethiopian elements. Some opponents were won to the pro-union side through terrorism, bribery, and promises of favoured treatment. The Eritrean Democratic Front, a new coalition composed of all the anti-union parties, was unable to prevent the Unionist Party from securing the appointment of an interim imperial representative in the territory, who in turn was able to use his influence to advance the unionist cause.

In accordance with the 1950 decision of the UN General Assembly, British military administration ended in September 1952 and was replaced by a new autonomous Eritrean government in federation with Ethiopia. The acquisition of the former Italian colony gave the ancient Ethiopian empire a coastline for the first time since the triumph of Islam over the African shore of the Red Sea in the 10th century AD. With a more advanced political structure than the rest of the empire, Eritrea had a desire for separatism that was bound to grow, so the federated status was undermined by the imperial government which would not tolerate an Eritrean-elected assembly or Eritrean control over police, local administration, and taxation. Eventually, the absence of adequate provisions for the creation of federal structures allowed Haile Selassie to succeed in reducing Eritrea's status to that of an Ethiopian province by 1962.

Eritrea under the Ethiopian Empire

Almost from the very start of federation the emperor's representatives began to undercut the territory's separate status under the federal system. In August 1955 Tedla Bairu, an Eritrean who was the leader of the Unionist Party and the chief executive elected by the Assembly, was replaced by an imperial nominee. Amharic was made the national language in place of Arabic and Tigrinya, and in 1959 the Eritrean flag was removed. In November 1962 with UN acquiescence, the Assembly, many of whose members had been accused of accepting bribes, voted unanimously to change Eritrea's status to that of a governorate (province). By that time the Assembly had been purged of all anti-annexation elements. Amid accusations of corruption and intimidation, Eritrea became Ethiopia's fourteenth province. All political parties were proscribed, censorship was imposed, the Amhara were given the top administrative positions, and the principle of parity between Christian and Muslim officials was abandoned. In an obvious attempt to 're-feudalize' the territory, an arch-imperialist, Ras Asrate Kassa, was appointed governor.

The extinction of the federation served to consolidate internal and external opposition to the union. Four years earlier in 1958 a number of Eritrean exiles, under the leadership of Hamid Idris Awate, had founded the Eritrean Liberation Movement in Cairo and this group shortly became the Eritrean Liberation Front (ELF). In addition to Hamid Idris, ELF leaders included Othman Salih Sabbe, former head of the Muslim League, and Woldeab Woldermariam, a Christian labour leader. As some urban Christians joined, the ELF became more radical, and even gained the support of Tedla Bairu. Initially a Muslim movement, the ELF was nationalistic rather than Marxist and received support from the Sudan and Ba'athist Syria. Later China (via South Yemen), Iraq, Somalia, Saudi Arabia and the Palestinian al-Fatah contributed. Local highway bands collected 'taxes' to help the movement. After 1961 the ELF turned to armed struggle and by 1966 was challenging the imperial forces throughout Eritrea.

In 1971 the ELF convened its First National Congress. Thereafter, the front articulated an anti-capitalist programme and created a forty-one-member Revolutionary Council. The Second National Congress of 1975, which reaffirmed the party's political direction, endorsed the leadership of Ahmed Nasser as chairman of the Revolutionary Council and his deputy, Ibrahim Toteel. The rapid growth of the ELF emphasized Eritrea's serious internal divisions. Divisions between urban and rural elements, socialists and nationalists, and Christians and Muslims were magnified as the ELF extended its operations and gained international publicity. Although differences within the Eritrean populace seriously diminished the ability of the guerrillas to wage war against the Ethiopian forces, they nevertheless posed a growing threat to the imperial government. In 1967 the government launched a massive military effort which led to tens of thousands of Eritreans crossing the border into the Sudan. In 1971 following the assassination of the provincial military commander, martial law was declared. The military confrontation between the Eritreans and the Ethiopian Government began in earnest.

In June 1970 Othman Salih Sabbe broke away from the ELF and formed the Eritrean People's Liberation Front (EPLF). The EPLF initially attracted a large number of urban, intellectual and leftist Christian youths and projected a strong socialist and nationalist image. The EPLF, a more radical and ideologically leftist group, attracted support from Libya, Iraq and Syria and published a monthly publication, *Vanguard*, in Tigrinya. However, a good measure of dissent was tolerated within the EPLF's ranks. A moderate wing led by Mohammed Nur Ed-Din Amin preferred to maintain a non-aligned status. The EPLF's strategy was to gain national independence through a protracted war. By 1975 it was estimated that it had more than 10,000 fighters in the field.

The growth of the EPLF was also accompanied by an intensification of conflict among the Eritreans themselves, particularly between 1972 and 1974 when casualties numbered well over 1,200. By 1976 yet another group was formed when Othman Salih Sabbe broke with the EPLF and formed the more pro-Western, pro-Arab Eritrean Liberation Front/Peoples' Liberation Forces (ELF-PLF), a division which partly reflected the differences between the fighters in Eritrea and their representatives abroad. The ELF-PLF realigned itself with the original ELF. However, after two phases of desertion from the ELF to the EPLF, first in 1977-78 and then in 1985 (following a second civil war), the ELF was left without a coherent military apparatus. Notwithstanding this, a number of disaffected factions remained loyal to the ELF, particularly those associated with Ahmed Nasser, the leader of a Soviet-leaning sub-group known as the Eritrean Liberation Front – Revolutionary Council (ELF-RC). Although a number of steps were taken to contain the secessionist movements, including the grouping of peasants in 'protected villages', not even the destructive conflict between the Eritrean groups could thwart the revolutionary momentum. Encouraged by the collapse of the imperial regime and its accompanying disorder, the guerrillas had succeeded in extending their control over the whole province by 1977. The Ethiopian forces were largely confined to urban centres and controlled the major roads only by day.

Eritrea after the Ethiopian Revolution

Following the 1974 revolution in Ethiopia and the assumption of power by the Derg (committee) under Mengistu Haile Mariam in 1977, the Ethiopian government continued to claim that Eritrea was part of Ethiopia. Initially, the Derg seemed to favour some form of true federation, and the Marxist opposition group in Addis Ababa espoused the Eritrean cause. Sharing a commitment to left wing ideology with the Derg, the Eritrean movements believed that a change of heart had occurred in Addis Ababa. Ultimately, however, the need to prevent any loss of territory or prestige drove the Derg to seek a military solution and the complete domination of Eritrea. The ELF-RC came under fire from the ELF and EPLF for allegedly carrying on secret negotiations with the Derg under Soviet sponsorship. The EPLF and ELF-PLF argued that the only effective and lasting negotiations would have to involve the United States, the Soviet Union and all rebel groups.

In May 1976 the Derg attempted to solve the Eritrean problem by again offering 'self-determination' to Eritrea if it joined a 'united revolutionary front'. When this offer was rejected by the Eritrean liberation movements, the Derg mobilized some 30,000 northern Ethiopian peasants, instructing them to take over Eritrea and promising them the conquered areas as their own. Eritrean forces quickly routed this untrained rabble, which became known as the 'peasant red march'. Another similar effort in April 1977 also failed and many died as a result of these 'solutions'.

In early 1977 Cuba became involved in north-east African affairs as an outgrowth of its close ties with the Soviet Union and their joint policy of assisting revolutionary regimes in Africa in the mid-1970s. United States military assistance to Ethiopia and its presence at bases in Eritrea ended in April 1977. Some time after, large numbers of Cuban and Soviet forces landed in Ethiopia and the Cuban defence minister Raul Castro visited Ethiopia, allegedly to co-ordinate military operations against the Somalis in the Ogaden desert. Cuban pilots were reportedly flying Soviet MIGs in this campaign. In a matter of weeks, the Somalis were driven out of the Ogaden with the assistance of an estimated 12,000 Cubans. By May 1977, when the Ethiopian government once more turned its attention to halting the secessionist movement in Eritrea, press reports were claiming that between 15,000 and 17,000 Cubans were part of the Ethiopian forces. This would have been Cuba's second largest contingent in Africa, following that stationed in Angola. A report on Cubans in Ethiopia of 30 May 1978 said the Cubans were reluctant to commit any troops to the offensive in Eritrea. However, later press items have indicated that some Cuban forces were involved in the area. A debate over the degree of Cuban involvement in Eritrea continues to this day.

Meanwhile, thousands of new recruits were joining the EPLF. Even greater numbers joined after the regime launched its 'Red Terror' campaign in Asmara, and following the capture of smaller provincial cities such as Keren and Dekamere (Decamhare) in late 1977. The armed struggle intensified and was eventually transformed into full-scale conventional warfare. By late 1978 the Eritrean resistance, which appeared to have won a number of battles and controlled virtually every urban centre except for Asmara and Massawa, was being steadily pushed out of the cities by heavy attacks organized by the Ethiopians and their Russian and Cuban advisers. The numerically and materially superior Ethiopian forces, armed mainly by the Soviets, achieved significant victories over the EPLF, which following defeat in the highlands, was forced to retreat to its stronghold in the north of Eritrea. Still, by mid-1979, partisan groups claimed to have repulsed a number of Ethiopian attacks and by early 1980 were reported to have opened a counter-offensive. It was clear by late April 1980, however, that all urban centres were in Ethiopian hands although guerrilla spokesmen claimed 'the countryside still belongs to the revolution'. The only northern town still believed to be under rebel control by that date was Nak'fa, but frequent clashes took place in the mountainous rural areas. Foreign observers reported the general feeling that a large-scale Ethiopian offensive was scheduled for the summer of 1980 as a final drive to crush the Eritrean rebellion.

On the diplomatic front, the Sudanese President Jaafar Mohammed Nimeiry, with the backing of Egypt's Anwar Sadat and Somalia's Mohammed Siad Barre, sought to mediate the conflict, primarily with the aim of shutting off any further flow of Eritrean refugees into the Sudan where 500,000 had already settled. Later, in the mid-1980s, the number of refugees was to soar even higher.

Nevertheless, the tide was turning in favour of the Eritreans. During Ethiopia's 'Red Star' offensive in 1982, which aimed to destroy all Eritrean resistance, the EPLF captured sufficient quantities of heavy artillery and tanks to transform it from a guerrilla force into a regular army. Throughout the mid-1980s the Ethiopian army was able to maintain its control over Eritrea's cities, while the liberation movements consolidated their hold over the countryside. Late in 1987 the EPLF went on the offensive, launching counter-attacks from secure bases throughout the late 1980s and slowly driving back the Ethiopian forces on all fronts. The Ethiopian army was forced to abandon all of northern Eritrea and the following year, 1988, all of the west fell to the Eritreans. Foreign aid workers were banned from Eritrea and Tigray, as the military situation deteriorated and the Mengistu regime continued its policy of trying to starve Eritrea into submission. Finally, after the failure of US-sponsored peace talks in the autumn of 1989, the EPLF captured the port of Massawa on the Red Sea and succeeded in severing a major supply route to the Ethiopian forces, who were by now besieged in Asmara. The Eritreans were able to strangle Ethiopia's routes to the sea, along which moved most of the Mengistu regime's trade and aid shipments. Food and humanitarian aid was routed through the Sudan to the EPLF instead of via the Ethiopian government. Throughout 1990 and 1991 the EPLF continued its success with several major victories over the Ethiopian army. In May 1991 after the Ethiopian troops had fled, units of the EPLF entered Asmara and immediately established an interim EPLF administration. With the collapse of Ethiopia's government, the EPLF proclaimed the *de facto* independence of Eritrea and formed a provisional government. Some 95,000 EPLF fighters and supporters worked to build a new government on a purely voluntary basis until formal recognition of the new government could be achieved.

Little by little, prominent exiles began to return. After fifteen years out of the country, Petros Makarios returned home to Eritrea in May 1991, as the country's new Coptic Orthodox bishop. The Coptic patriarch in Egypt dispatched him with the additional task of establishing a separate Eritrean Orthodox Church, distinct from that of Ethiopia. Another returnee was Sultan Alimirah of the Afar, who had sought to unite and stabilize the Danakil region, in spite of its division among Eritrea, Ethiopia and Djibouti and his own seventeen-year absence in exile.

Independent Eritrea

Following the liberation of Asmara by the EPLF, and of Addis Ababa by the Ethiopian People's Revolutionary Democratic Front (EPRDF), a conference was convened in London in August 1991, under the chairmanship of the United States Assistant Secretary of State for African Affairs. Representatives of the EPLF attended as a separate delegation from the EPRDF, which was now in control of Ethiopia and sympathetic to Eritrean nationalist aspirations. During the conference, the United States and the Ethiopian delegation both accepted the EPLF administration as the legitimate provisional government of Eritrea, and the EPLF agreed to hold a referendum on independence in 1993. No other organizations were invited to participate, though the EPLF promised that free elections would be held following the referendum. The provisional government that was to administer Eritrea during the two years prior to the referendum drew most of its members from within the ranks of the EPLF.

The United Nations supervised referendum on Eritrean independence was held between the 23 and 25 April 1993; of the 1,102,410 Eritreans who voted, 99.8 per cent endorsed national independence. The anniversary of the EPLF's triumphant entry into Asmara, the 24 May, was proclaimed Independence Day, and on 28 May, Eritrea became the 182nd member of the United Nations. In the following month the new nation was admitted to the Organization of African Unity (OAU). Eritrea was also accorded diplomatic recognition by a substantial number of countries, including Ethiopia and its other neighbours, Egypt, Israel, Syria, Russia, the People's Republic of China, the United States of America, Italy, and other European states.

The new nation's flag consists of a rectangular field, green at the top and light blue at the bottom, with a red triangle, its base corresponding to the hoist and its apex at the centre of the fly. Inside the triangle is a vertical gold olive branch surrounded by a wreath of gold olive branches.

Since the referendum, which was also endorsed by those groups opposed to the EPLF, the latter has maintained its pre-eminent position in the transitional administration of Eritrea. Following Eritrea's formal accession to independence, a four-year transitional period was declared, during which preparations were to proceed for establishing a constitutional and pluralist political system. At the apex of the transitional government were three state institutions: the Consultative Council (the executive authority composed of the cabinet ministers, provincial administrators and heads of government authorities and commissions); the National Assembly (the legislature formed from the Central Committee of the EPLF with the addition of thirty members from the Provincial Assemblies and an additional thirty individuals selected by the Central Committee); and the judiciary. The government also established a commission to initiate the drafting of a constitution. One of the National Assembly's first acts was the election of a head of state. Unsurprisingly, Issaias Afewerki, the EPLF's Secretary General was elected by a vote of ninety-nine to five in May 1993.

Although the EPLF-led provisional government has professed its commitment to democracy, political stability and the rebuilding of the country have been given priority. In addition, some Eritreans have spoken out against the EPLF's continued monopoly of political power and its almost total control of the economy and media. Indeed, several prominent Muslim leaders and their supporters said that they would not return from exile unless their rights to engage in organized political activity were fully guaranteed. The Danakil of southern Eritrea whose land is now split between Eritrea and Ethiopia, have pressed for their own independent homeland.

The euphoria surrounding independence has given way to the full realization of the country's serious economic and social problems. The most daunting task facing the new government was the need to rehabilitate and develop Eritrea's war-torn economy and infrastructure, and to feed a population of whom eighty per cent remained severely disrupted by the war. Urban economic activity was almost non-existent. The government was confronted by the additional problem of how to reintegrate some 750,000 refugees, of whom approximately 500,000 lived in Sudan, mostly at subsistence level. Increases in rents, and the prices of medicines, water and electricity were introduced in June 1993 and were reported to have provoked strong resentment among residents of Asmara.

At its third congress, held in Asmara in mid-February 1994, the EPLF debated its own dissolution and decided to transform itself into a political party, called the People's Front for Democracy and Justice. An eighteen-member Executive Committee and a seventy-five-member Central Committee were elected; President Afewerki was elected Chairman of the latter. In early March 1994 a fourth session of the National Assembly adopted a series of resolutions, including an amendment whereby the former executive body, the Consultative Council, was to be superseded by a sixteen-member cabinet. Former government authorities with responsibility for transport and tourism were to be upgraded to ministerial level. Other measures adopted by resolutions of the Assembly included the creation of a forty-two-member Constitutional Commission, and the establishment of a committee charged with the re-organization of the country's administrative divisions.

External relations have proved problematic. The transitional government has attempted to consolidate good relations with Eritrea's neighbours and to develop stronger links with the United States of America, China and other major powers. This has generally been successful, in spite of Eritrean criticism of American involvement in Somalia. Eritrea was admitted to the United Nations in May 1993 and joined the Organization of African Unity the following month. The country has also established close relationships with its African neighbours the Sudan, Ethiopia, and Djibouti and with its neighbours across the Red Sea, Yemen and Saudi Arabia. Relations between Eritrea and Ethiopia remain exceedingly complex as both mutual fears and the need for co-operation are recognized. Eritrea's central role in the overthrow of Mengistu is recognized and appreciated by most Ethiopians. Pending the full establishment of its own monetary system, Eritrea continues to use the Ethiopian unit of currency, the birr. Strong economic ties with Ethiopia are expected, especially in the light of a 1992 agreement whereby Ethiopia would continue to have full use of the Eritrean port of Assab for its imports and exports. Nevertheless, the obstacles are numerous. Air transport between Eritrea and Ethiopia has been difficult due to heavy demand and rumours that Eritreans were to take over Ethiopian Airlines have abounded, to the alarm of many Ethiopians, who often see their northern neighbours as grasping and vengeful.

Another source of tension between Eritreans and Ethiopians were accusations that the EPLF had mistreated Ethiopian prisoners of war during the period of the final drive on Asmara in 1991. Claims of summary executions were made, but neglect due to scarce resources seems to have played a greater role. Issaias Afewerki's victorious return to his home in Afabet was marred by the sombre spectacle of his vehicle weaving among the bloated bodies of hundreds of Ethiopian soldiers who had died of hunger and thirst. Some 60,000 other Ethiopians who had been living in Eritrea also fled south and established shanty towns on the outskirts of Addis Ababa.

In late September 1993 the first meeting of the Ethiopian-Eritrean joint ministerial commission was held in Asmara, during which an agreement was reached on measures to allow the free movement of nationals between each country, and on co-operation regarding foreign affairs and economic policy. Meetings held between the Eritrean President and the Ethiopian President, Meles Zenawi, in December underlined the good relations prevailing between the two governments and their efforts to co-ordinate policy with regard to Somalia. Earlier the same year, in June, the OAU had appointed President Afewerki to work towards solving the Somalia problem, an appointment supported by the United Nations Security Council and other member states of the UN.

The complexity of regional relations, and of Eritrea's position, became evident in July 1993, when, during a visit to Saudi Arabia, the Eritrean President had to counter allegations that Israel was establishing a military presence in Eritrea. Prior to the referendum, harsh reactions had been provoked in the Arab press after Afewerki visited Israel for medical treatment. The Eritrean government is keen to maintain good relations with its Arab neighbours, but not to the detriment of what it regards as important ties with Israel. It is interesting to note that Saudi Arabia had previously provided support to the ELF, the EPLF's rival.

Relations between Eritrea and the Sudan, which had supported the EPLF during the war, deteriorated in late December 1993, following an incursion by members of a Muslim fundamentalist group into Eritrea from the Sudan. In a clash with Eritrean forces, all the members of the group, and an Eritrean commander, were killed. In response to the incident, the Eritrean President stressed the links between the extremist opposition group, the Eritrean Islamic Jihad, and the Sudanese National Islamic Front, led by Dr Hassan el Turabi, implying that the latter had possessed full prior knowledge of the incursion. However, following a swift denial by the Sudanese Government that it would ever interfere in the affairs of neighbouring states, the Eritrean President reaffirmed his support for the Sudanese authorities and his commitment to improving bilateral relations. In August 1993 it was reported that the Eritrean Islamic Jihad had split between its political wing, led by Sheikh Mohammed Arafa, and a military wing, the former having been accused by the latter of inefficiency and of establishing secret contacts with the government in Asmara.

In mid-1992 the Eritrean army was composed mainly of the forces of the Eritrean People's Liberation Front, which were estimated to number about 85,000 men and women. These forces possess a vast array of modern weapons, many of them captured when the EPLF drove the remnants of the Ethiopian army from Asmara in May 1991.

The provisional government promised to reduce the size of the army once the stability of the country was assured and by late 1993, some 26,000 combatants (those who had joined after 1990) had been demobilized. Military service has been made compulsory for all Eritreans between the ages of eighteen and forty for a period of twelve to eighteen months. The Eritrean army has a major task in detecting and disposing of land mines laid by both sides in the war. The mines have hampered agriculture and are thought to have maimed more than 11,000 people.

The Eritrean authorities are believed to have assumed control of the Ethiopian navy, based in the ports of Massawa and Assab. This includes a naval college staffed by Norwegians which was established at Massawa in 1955, with a training centre for support personnel at Dongolo Gend. Since 1958, a number of patrol boats have acted as a coast guard unit off the Eritrean coast and a used seaplane tender and some landing crafts were acquired from the United States as part of the Military Assistance Programme in the early 1960s. The first commodore was Eskender Desta, Haile Selassie's grandson, who was shot in 1974. Some Soviet equipment was also purchased or donated in the 1980s, but the current size and operational capability of the Eritrean navy is unclear at this time. The navy's principal function has always been to patrol the country's waters in search of illegal fishing activity by foreign operators.

Eritrea's economy

There is little statistical information available on the Eritrean economy, but it is estimated that Eritrea is one of the poorest countries in Africa, with an annual income of between US $75 and US $150 per capita. Although Eritrea has the distinction of being one of the very few non-debtor states in Africa, many of its people are without even a subsistence income. At the end of the war in 1991 it was estimated that more than eighty-five per cent of the population were surviving on international relief. The need for the government to redevelop the economy is, therefore, the greatest challenge facing the country. In 1993 it was estimated that it would cost about $3,000,000,000 to begin the reconstruction of the economy and infrastructure. However, in 1992, according to the government relief co-ordination office, Eritrea received less than $32,000,000 in overseas aid. In 1993 Eritrea was included on the European Community's list of countries in severe difficulties which would benefit from a fund of 100,000,000 ECUs in aid for rehabilitation programmes, but these programmes have yet to be established.

Furthermore, as of early 1994 there has been virtually no foreign investment in the country.

Eritrea is a predominantly agrarian nation, with about seventy-five per cent of the population depending on farming and pastoralism for a livelihood. A variety of crops are grown in different agro-climatic regions. Sedentary agriculturists living in the higher, cooler, and wetter regions of the country depend primarily on the cultivation of grains. These include wheat, barley, teff (a staple grain indigenous to Eritrea and Ethiopia), sorghum, and pulses. Some livestock, such as oxen, are raised for use in farming while sheep, goats, donkeys, camels and chickens are also reared. Agro-pastoralists living in the lower and hotter areas, where precipitation is sporadic, depend on both livestock raising and the cultivation of crops, including maize, sorghum, millet, cotton, and sesame seed. Livestock raising is the principal means of livelihood for pastoralists living in the semi-dry and dry sections of Eritrea's lowland areas.

The agricultural economy suffered considerable disruption during the thirty years of war, especially in the western lowlands and the northern mountains and lowland regions, where most of the fighting took place. The war also disrupted agricultural activity in the more productive and densely populated highland areas. Additionally, Eritrean agriculturalists have suffered the effects of some two decades of inadequate rainfall, unpredictable climatic conditions, and periodic locust infestations. Indeed, the total food production declined by about forty per cent between 1980 and 1990. Food shortages have been severe, and in 1993 a massive three-quarters of Eritrea's population was dependent on foreign assistance to meet daily food requirements.

The new national government has taken several steps to rehabilitate the agricultural sector. In an effort to stimulate production, the Eritrean authorities have exempted agricultural (and industrial) exports from sales tax, although they will continue to be subject to export duty. In 1992, agricultural production increased fourfold after modest amounts of seeds, fertilizer, and oxen were provided to farmers, and copious rainfall gave rise to the hope that the long drought might be ending. Efforts were begun to rehabilitate the large commercial farms that had lain fallow during the long war of independence. That year some 315,000 hectares of land were cultivated and the harvest was good enough to satisfy an estimated fifty-four per cent of Eritrea's food requirements. The grain harvest increased from some 70,000 metric tons in 1991 to between 250,000 and 300,000 tons in 1992, but 1993 was a disastrous year, following the almost complete failure of the rains and the persistent problems caused by crop pests. As a result, eighty per cent of the grain crop was estimated to have been lost, and there was a cereal deficit of about 190,000 tons. Much of the country required emergency food aid. In June 1993 the World Food Programme announced the beginning of a six-month emergency food operation to assist more than half a million Eritreans suffering serious food shortages. Given the country's new-found stability, the future is likely to be brighter than the present. However, a lack of animal power, seed grains and capital equipment will certainly hamper the long-term development of the agricultural sector. In 1993 there were only forty-seven tractors in the entire country.

Much of Eritrea's wooded land has been destroyed to make space for settlement and cultivation, and to provide firewood. This meant that by 1993 forests accounted for only 1.1 per cent of Eritrea's total land area. Serious environmental degradation, caused directly and indirectly by the war, also presents a huge problem. Owing to the problem of water scarcity and unreliable rainfall, careful water management and conservation are essential. In 1992, seventeen water reservoirs, twenty small earthen dams, numerous ponds and hundreds of kilometres of irrigation ditches were built as part of environmental rehabilitation programmes. In an attempt to prevent soil erosion, more than 40,000 kilometres of badly eroded hillsides have been terraced and 22,000,000 new trees have been planted.

Spurred by prompt action by the government, nearly all of the forty or so state-owned industries that stood idle during the war were operating at one-third capacity in 1991 and either fully or partially by 1993. Eritrea's small industrial sector produces batteries, beer, cement, edible oils, glass, kitchen utensils, leather goods, matches, textiles and canned meat and fish. The industrial sector is believed to require at least an initial US $30,000,000 of capital investment in order to begin operating to capacity. The government has calculated that the cost of industrial recovery would be $20,000,000 for the private sector and $66,000,000 for the state sector.

Although the government has stated that its aim is to create a free-market economy, there has, as yet, been little international aid provided by large bilateral donors such as the United States of America. Suspicions aroused by the ruling party's former Marxist ideology are believed to have been one factor in this delay. The government controlled nearly all industrial output in 1993, but it has promised to move towards privatizing industry. A new investment code has been issued, which prescribes tax allowances on income, low import and export duties for up to five years, and duty-free imports of materials required to establish industrial enterprises. In a further effort to encourage foreign investment and the development of a free market, the government has guaranteed that assets will not be nationalized or confiscated, prices will not be fixed and the State will not hold monopolies.

The Provisional Government of Eritrea estimated that at least $2 billion in outside assistance was required to replenish the country's bankrupt treasury and build a viable economy. The World Bank pledged $147 million in 1992, and Eritrea received about $32 million from the United Nations and other non-governmental organizations. In addition, several Western nations provided financial aid, but the donations did not begin to approach what was needed. Remittances from the large community of expatriate Eritreans, many of whom have settled in Europe, North America, and the Middle East, provided a substantial amount of Eritrea's hard currency. However, without an elected government or a free-market economy, Eritrea has been slow to attract substantial foreign investment. Aside from the lack of investment, two major structural problems hamper the expansion of Eritrea's manufacturing base: the lack of local demand for all but the most basic manufactures; and the absence of domestic energy resources. Unless reserves of petroleum or natural gas are discovered off shore, Eritrea will have to import all of its energy needs.

With a 600-mile Red Sea coastline, Eritrea has immense potential to harvest fish for local consumption and export. As many as 250 species, including salmon, sardines, tuna, anchovies, barracuda, sea pike, shark, cod, shrimp, and lobster, have been identified around the Dahlak archipelago alone. Sardines are the leading commercial species. In 1993 the United Nations, as well as some European non-governmental organizations, provided some financial assistance to train Eritreans in new fishing techniques and equipment-making. Fisheries are a real potential growth area for the Eritrean economy and have been given serious consideration by both the government and aid donors. In addition, a Food and Agriculture Organization-sponsored conference was held in Massawa in March 1993 to discuss measures to develop Eritrea's marine fishery resources. The Eritrean government views the development of the fishing industry as vitally important, given the country's chronic shortage of protein and the acceptance of fish in both Christian and Muslim diets.

Foreign investors were also being sought in 1993 to build tourist facilities. Concurrently, the government was renovating hotels in Asmara and in the port cities of Massawa and Assab to attract tourists.

Like fishing and tourism, mining remained a largely untapped source of economic development in the early 1990s. Eritrea's mineral resources are believed to be of significant potential value. Of particular importance, in view of Eritrea's acute energy shortage, is the possibility of locating large reserves of petroleum and natural gas beneath the Red Sea. In early 1993 the Government made petroleum exploration regulations more stringent and British Petroleum, which had signed a contract for petroleum exploration with the former Ethiopian regime, had its exploration rights invalidated. The United States petroleum company, Amoco, and the International Petroleum Corporation of Canada are the only two remaining companies with concessions. The latter has operating rights in the 31,000 square kilometre Danakil block along the Eritrean coast, where there are believed to be good prospects for petroleum and gas discoveries. However, the two companies are still waiting for the legal status of their contracts, signed under the Mengistu regime, to be determined. Until they are, little further exploration is likely to take place.

Eritrea is reported to have considerable reserves of iron, marine salt, gold, copper, nickel and potash, with gold-bearing seams existing in many of the igneous rocks forming the highlands of Eritrea. There are at least fifteen gold mines and a large number of prospects close to Asmara, and the potential for new discoveries in the country is considered good. In the vicinity of Barentu, 150 kilometres west of Asmara, there is also a region of widespread gold mining potential. Furthermore, chromites, kaolin, manganese, titanium, mica, and magnesium are known to exist in small quantities.

Unemployment is estimated to affect as many as fifty per cent of the labour force. One of the major problems facing the government has been the need to occupy thousands of EPLF fighters now that the war is ended; in the short term, most of them have been employed on 'food-for-work' schemes and involved in public works such as constructing roads and terracing hillsides. However, in May 1993 the former soldiers staged a demonstration, motivated by concerns over lack of pay and their poor living conditions. Although the demonstration was non-violent and orderly, it drew the government's attention to the precarious position of, on the one hand, being unable to demobilize the fighters unless there was sufficient work for them, and on the other hand, having to employ them without pay, possibly for another year or two.

In March 1993 the International Development Association approved a credit of SDR 18,100,000 (US $25,000,000) to support Eritrea's $147,000,000 two-year Recovery and Rehabilitation Programme, which was to be funded by a series of loans on concessionary terms. The second largest contributor was Italy, which pledged $24,300,000. Contributions were also promised by a number of other European countries, the European Union and the United Nations Development Programme. The main components of the programme were: agricultural and industrial input; equipment for infrastructural development; mechanical, electrical and telecommunications spare parts; construction materials for the infrastructure and cottage industries; and support for administration and economic planning.

Steps towards international economic integration were taken in May 1993, when Eritrea was admitted to the group of African, Caribbean and Pacific (ACP) countries party to the Lomé Convention. In September an International Monetary Fund (IMF) delegation visited Asmara and held talks with the government regarding Eritrea's application to join the Fund. The following month, an Eritrean delegation was invited to attend the joint World Bank-IMF annual meeting in Washington. Eritrea is eager to show the international donor community its commitment to implementing a liberal trade and exchange regime and to developing an export-oriented domestic economy. As early as January 1992 Eritrea and Ethiopia signed an agreement whereby the port of Assab became a free port for Ethiopia, and which provided for tax-free trade between the two countries, using the Ethiopian birr as currency. International donors are fully aware that the future of Eritrea's economy will very much depend on economic relations with Ethiopia.

Infrastructure

Eritrea has a relatively well-developed network of roads, including 300 miles of asphalt and several thousand miles of other all-weather roads. Over 1,000 miles of all-weather feeder roads were built by the EPLF during the liberation struggle. Many of the major roads, however, have fallen into disrepair from decades of neglect and war damage. The road between Massawa and Asmara has now been rebuilt. In addition, a railroad, about 180 miles long, connects the port of Massawa with the capital, Asmara, and then continues north to the second largest city, Keren, and west to Agordat, the principal town of the western administrative district of the same name near the Sudanese border. However, damage to the railway throughout the long war for independence was so great that there is some doubt as to whether it will ever be operational again.

Eritrea's Red Sea ports, Massawa and Assab, provide important sea links with the outside world. Massawa sustained severe damage during the war, but by 1993 most of the damaged facilities had been repaired, rendering the port almost fully operational. Assab has little transit value for Eritrea because of its distance from the country's northern hinterland, but may prove to be important for Ethiopian transit trade in the future. Eritrea's merchant navy numbers fourteen ships.

The Italian colonial rule left Eritrea with a high level of illiteracy. Education was extended to only a handful of children of urban Eritreans, and the highest level of schooling an Eritrean could attain after 1933 was primary. The British, during their eleven-year administrative tenure, increased the number of primary schools from twenty-four to one hundred, and also opened a number of middle and secondary schools, predominantly in urban areas. During the federation period (1952-62), the Ethiopian government made education accessible in some rural areas, but the situation began to deteriorate after the Ethiopian annexation of Eritrea in 1962. For many years education in much of the country, especially the lowland areas, came to a standstill due to war activity. This situation began to change somewhat in the late 1970s and 1980s as the EPLF liberated much of the countryside and a number of towns from Ethiopian occupation. Although hampered by shortages of teachers, teaching materials, and equipment, the EPLF managed to open and operate several hundred schools in the liberated areas.

A massive literacy campaign was launched in the early 1980s and by 1990 illiteracy was reduced by as much as seventy per cent in some areas. Women were the greatest beneficiaries of this programme because traditionally women had little or no access to any form of education in much of lowland Eritrea. The EPLF also opened more than a dozen primary schools in the Sudan for some of the 500,000 Eritrean refugees living in Khartoum, Kassala, and Port Sudan and in rural settlements in the eastern Sudan. The overall rate of adult illiteracy in Eritrea is estimated to be eighty per cent, with the rate among former women fighters believed to be as high as ninety-five per cent.

In the first two years after the EPLF victory, all Eritrean schools were re-opened and many war-damaged buildings were repaired. Education materials were being prepared in all Eritrean languages. Education, which is not compulsory, is provided free of charge in government schools. There are also some fee-paying private schools. Owing to the severe disruption the war caused to many people's education, there are no strict age-groups at any particular level. However, as an approximate guide, nursery education begins at four years of age, primary is from six to ten years of age, junior is from ten to thirteen years of age, and secondary is from thirteen to seventeen years of age. Many educated veterans of the war of independence have worked as teachers without pay.

Similarly, Eritreans returned from exile to teach at Asmara University (renamed the University of Eritrea) for little or no salary. In 1992-93 the university, which did not charge students for tuition, food or housing, had 3,250 students and 106 members of the teaching staff. Some 14,000 people had applied for about 1,600 places in the first year of 1993-94. Shortages of staff, books, laboratory equipment, classrooms, and dormitories remained a problem and the university was forced to close again in 1994 although it has now re-opened.

A good number of hospitals and clinics were built during the Italian colonial era, but the effects of war have severely stretched the capabilities of the country's health services. In the early 1990s the infant mortality rate was estimated to be 135 per 1,000 live births, average life expectancy at birth was forty-six years, and the population per physician was 48,000. An estimated 60,000 children have been left cripples by the war, and another 45,000 orphaned. Medical facilities remain extremely limited.

Women's issues have proved to be prominent in Eritrean life. During the war for independence, thousands of Eritrean women took up arms against both the Empire and the Derg. To the inhabitants of neighbouring countries, Eritrean women tend to be characterized as alarmingly liberated. However, a good deal of evidence suggests that their status, politically and socially, has declined since the fighting stopped. One enduring and controversial issue related to women is that of female genital mutilation, since both male and female infants are circumcised by Eritrean and Ethiopian Christians, Muslims, Jews, and some animists. The age for the operation ranges from five days after birth for Amhara girls (seven day for males) to seven years of age among the Beni Amer (who do not circumcise girls). In some groups, girls are circumcised at birth, whilst in others the operation takes place between the ages of eight and ten, and still others at anytime before age twelve. The rationale for clitoridectomy (excision of a girl's clitoris) is that it will help to preserve her virginity until marriage and discourage her from faithlessness afterwards. The Mensa ensure virginity by infibulation, or the partial sewing up the vaginal opening. Needless to say, health problems are the consequences for many women. Efforts to abolish female genital mutilation have failed in the face of strong tradition.

Conclusions

Eritrea remains a land of both bright prospects and severe difficulties. The unity and national spirit fostered during the thirty years of armed struggle is being rerouted into efforts to cope with a desperately poor economic situation and a deteriorating environment. Much remains to be done. However, given the enthusiasm with which solutions are being explored, there is reason to be optimistic as long as the nation's diverse ethnic and religious groups remain co-operative, reasonably stable relations with the country's neighbours are maintained and the government promotes policies of inclusiveness.

Names and Orthography

The naming of ethnic groups, languages and nationalities is a matter of some confusion. The transliteration of both Ethiopic and Arabic names remains a matter of some debate.

The place-names associated with Eritrea were generally standardized in the colonial era, although there are some differences between Italian and British usage. I have used the most common forms of place-names, rather than attempting to uniformly apply one system or another.

Personal names in both Arabic and Eritrean languages appear in forms based on those tongues, with Arabic names listed alphabetically by first name, if no family name appears, and Eritrean and Ethiopian names listed according to family names, which usually appear as the first name. However, some confusion has developed as a number of scholars and other prominent figures from the Horn of Africa have reversed the order of their names to adapt to Western norms.

The Country and Its People

1 **Birth of a nation.**
Anonymous. Asmara: Government of Eritrea, 1993. 44p.
Because Eritrea only gained its independence in the early 1990s, there is a lack of book-length, general sources on the country. This publication of the Eritrean Ministry of External Affairs provides a good overview of the country and represents a starting point, particularly for those studying Eritrean history, politics and geography.

2 **Country report: Eritrea.**
Anonymous. *The Courier* (July/August 1994), p. 9-27.
The *Courier* is UNESCO's own magazine and this special edition contains six articles on Eritrea, dealing with the topics of: reconstruction; repatriation of refugees; co-operation with the European Union; political developments and foreign relations; women's issues and the rebuilding of the port of Massawa.

Eritrea.
See item no. 323.

A historical dictionary of Ethiopia and Eritrea.
See item no. 324.

Travel Guides

3 **Guida dell'Africa Orientale Italiana.** (Guide to Italian East Africa).
Consociazione Turistica Italiana.   Milan: Stampato nelle Officine
Fotolitografiche SA, 1938. 640p.

Though dated, this official guidebook to Italian East Africa (Eritrea, Ethiopia and
Somalia) is one of the most thorough ever produced. Of particular interest to
travellers and historians today, it contains numerous photographs and forty-one maps.
Another interesting guide from the colonial era is *Etiopia, Eritrea, Somalia* (Ethiopia,
Eritrea, Somalia) by Umberto Ademollo (Milan: Touring Club Italiano, 1934. 37p.).
This short booklet is available on microfilm.

4 **East African handbook.**
Michael Hodd.   Chicago: Passport Books, 1994. 864p.

This guidebook is the best current source of information for travellers bound for
Eritrea. The chapter on Eritrea (p. 620-36) contains background data on the country's
geography, climate, history, cultures, politics and economy. Detailed information on
Asmara includes a brief introduction to the city, places of interest, accommodation,
restaurants, banks, shopping, diplomatic missions, entertainment, post offices,
religious institutions, tourist offices and transport. Further information is presented on
the Massawa-Agordat railway, Dekamere, Keren, Agordat, Massawa, Assab and the
Dahlak Marine National Park. The chapter concludes with four pages of information
for visitors (entry requirements, best times to visit, health, money, transport to
Eritrea, calendar, customs, electricity, business hours, time, religion, weights and
measures, accommodation, food and drink, transport within Eritrea, language,
newspapers, radio, television, holidays and festivals, and further reading). Maps of
Eritrea and central Asmara are also included.

5   **Eritrea: a tourist guide.**
Robert Papstein.   Lawrenceville, New Jersey: Red Sea Press, 1995.
128p.
This is the most recent guide devoted solely to Eritrea. Also good is Edward Paice's *Guide to Eritrea* (Chalfont St. Peter, England: Bradt; Old Saybrook, Connecticut: Globe Pequot, 1994. 166p.)

6   **A handbook on Eritrea.**
Anonymous.   Asmara: British Ministry of Information for Eritrea,
[1944]. 36p.
This is an old, but interesting, guidebook to Eritrea for tourists and other visitors. Particularly interesting is the description of the career of Baron Werner von Münzinger, a Swiss who served as both the British and French consul in Massawa, married an Eritrean woman, and then in 1872 led an Egyptian expedition which attempted to conquer Ethiopia from Eritrea. The guide was reprinted and expanded by ten pages by the British Information Services sometime in the early 1950s.

Explorers' and Travellers' Accounts

Before 1800

7   **The Prester John of the Indies.**
    F. Alvarez.   London: Hakluyt Society, 1961. 617p.

Mediaeval Europeans believed that beyond the Muslim-dominated Middle East was the legendary kingdom of Prester John, a Christian realm waiting to be reconnected with the rest of Christendom. With this in mind, the Portuguese reached the Eritrean coast in the early 1500s and made contact with the Abyssinian rulers of that time. Lord Stanley of Alderley translated and C. F. Beckingham and G. W. B. Huntingford edited this Portuguese explorer/missionary's account of Eritrea and Ethiopia in the 16th century. Comments on the legend of Prester John are included. This work, which includes illustrations and maps, has appeared in both one- and two-volume formats and was reprinted by Kraus (Nendeln, Liechtenstein) in 1975. Lord Stanley also translated and edited Alvarez's *Narrative of the Portuguese Embassy to Abyssinia* (London: Hakluyt Society, 1881. 416p.), which chronicles events from 1520 to 1527. It was reprinted by B. Franklin Publishers of New York in 1970. A good book on the Prester John legends is *The land of Prester John: a chronicle of Portuguese exploration* by Elaine Sanceau (New York: Knopf, 1944. 243p.).

8   **Some records of Ethiopia.**
    C. F. Beckingham, G. W. B. Huntingford.   London: Hakluyt Society, 1954. 267p.

This collection includes a great deal of information on Eritrea. Particularly interesting is Manoel de Almeida's *The history of high Ethiopia*. Illustrations and maps accompany the book, which was reprinted by Kraus (Nendeln, Liechtenstein) in 1967.

9 Travels to discover the sources of the Nile in the years 1768-1773.
   James Bruce. Edinburgh: J. Ruthven, 1790. 5 vols.

James Bruce was the first of the great British travellers to popularize African exploration in the Western world. He describes the history and natural environment of Eritrea in the first volume of this work. The 1805 edition of Bruce's account, published in Edinburgh by Murray, includes a biographical note on Bruce by Henry Salt. An abridged edition of 281 pages, edited by C. F. Beckingham, was published by Edinburgh University Press in 1964.

10 The Suma oriental of Tome Pires.
    Armando Cortesao. London: Hakluyt Society, 1944. Reprinted,
    Nendeln: Kraus, 1967. 2 vols.

This is an account of Tome Pires's voyage from the Red Sea to India and Malacca between 1512 and 1515. It includes plates and maps and was reprinted by Kraus (Nendeln, Liechtenstein) in 1967.

11 Ethiopian itineraries circa 1400-1524.
    Edited by O. G. S. Crawford. London: Hakluyt Society, 1958. 231p.
    bibliog.

Crawford's collection includes illustrations, maps and a particularly good work by the Venetian, Alessandro Zorzi, who travelled in Eritrea from 1519 to 1524. An eleven-page bibliography is found in the front material.

12 The Red Sea and adjacent countries.
    Edited by W. Foster. London: Hakluyt Society, 1949. 192p.

This collection of travellers' accounts from the end of the 17th and early 18th centuries includes C. J. Poncet's 1709 work, A voyage to Aethiopia and Ovington's notes on Red Sea ports. It was reprinted by Kraus (Nendeln, Liechtenstein) in 1967.

13 Abysinnia and its people.
    John Camden Hotten. New York: Negro Universities Press, 1969.
    384p. bibliog.

Originally published in 1868 by the author, this reprint consists of a collection of excerpts from twenty-three travellers' accounts, ranging from that of Alvarez in 1520 to Dr Charles Beke's description of 1865. These are followed by: British Consul Plowden's description of Abyssinia in 1852-55; a narrative on the British subjects held captive by Ethiopian Emperor Theodore (Tewodros); suggestions for a military expedition; and an excellent, though haphazardly arranged bibliography. Eritrea features prominently in the accounts of James Bruce, the French Expedition of 1839-43 and Manfield Parkyns, as well as in four of the five suggested invasion routes in part four.

14 A voyage to Abyssinia.
    Jerónimo (Jerome) Lobo, translated by Samuel Johnson. London:
    Bettesworth & Hitch, 1735. 396p.

This is Samuel Johnson's 1735 English translation of Le Grand's 1673 French translation of the 1669 original Portuguese journals of the Jesuit Father Lobo. Lobo's

17th-century travels in the Horn of Africa with fellow Jesuit Pedro Paez are significant in the early history of Eritrea and provide descriptive accounts of the region's history, religious practices, customs and natural history. The legends of Prester John and of mythical animals are also found in Lobo's writings. Reprints were made of this work in 1814 and 1887. A more easily accessible account is *The itinerario of Jeronimo Lobo*, translated by Donald M. Lockhart from the Portuguese text and edited by M. Goncalves da Costa (London: Hakluyt Society, 1984. 417p.).

15 Travellers in Ethiopia.

Richard Pankhurst. London: Oxford University Press, 1965. 147p. bibliog.

This excellent, short anthology includes extracts from the accounts of many of the travellers mentioned in this section as well as from *The Periplus of the Erythraean Sea* and *The Christian topography of Cosmas Indicopleustes*. Introductory notes precede each excerpt. Together with a number of photographs and maps, this book includes a six-page bibliography.

16 The Periplus of the Erythraean Sea.

Translated by W. H. Schoff. New York: Longman, Green & Co., 1912. 323p.

Early trade between the Mediterranean world and the lands around the Indian Ocean is described in this ancient Greek account and trading manual. Seasonal reversals of the monsoon winds made it possible to develop sail-borne trade between the Red Sea and India before the first century AD. The manual describes places, events, products and conditions in the lands along these routes, including Eritrea. Gold, spices and textiles were the principal items of trade and the ancient Eritrean port of Adulis was a key stopping point on this route. This is an English translation of the original Greek text, with maps and a short bibliography added. A good related work is J. W. McCrindle's translation of *The Christian topography of Cosmas Indicopleustes* (London: Hakluyt Society, 1897).

17 Travels of the Jesuits in Ethiopia.

Balthazar Telles, translated by John Stevens. In: *A new collection of travels and voyages*. London: J. Knapton, A. Bell & J. Baker, 1710. 264p. 2 vols.

Originally appearing in monthly issues, this account of a Portuguese Jesuit priest was translated by British Captain John Stevens and appears in volume two of the main work. It describes the geography and history of Eritrea, Ethiopia, Yemen and Afar country. The author's name is variously spelt Telles or Tellez.

18 The Portuguese expedition to Abyssinia in 1541-53, as narrated by Castanhoso.

Edited by R. S. Whiteway. London: Hakluyt Society, 1902. 296p.

This work is particularly good in detailing the relationships between the Portuguese and states in the Horn of Africa in the mid-16th century, a time when the Portuguese were aiding the Abyssinian Christian rulers against their Muslim enemies. Much of the book consists of translations of correspondence from that era. There is a folding map in a pocket.

La Mer Rouge: l'Abyssinie et l'Arabie aux XVIe et XVIIe siècles et la cartographie des portulans du monde orientale. (The Red Sea: Abyssinia and Arabia in the 16th and 17th centuries and the Portuguese cartography of the eastern world).
See item no. 44.

A new history of Ethiopia.
See item no. 106.

19th century

19 **A journey through Abyssinia.**
Henry Dufton.   Westport, Connecticut: Negro Universities Press, 1970. 337p.
The twelfth chapter of this volume, which was reprinted from the 1867 original (published by Chapman & Hall in London), deals with the author's journey in 1862-63 from the Ethiopian interior to Massawa. In common with numerous other travellers, Dufton journeyed up the Nile, over the Abyssinian plateau and ended his adventures on the Eritrean coast. His descriptions and maps offer information on the region in the mid-19th century.

20 **Assab e i Danachili: viaggio e studii.** (Assab and the Danakil: journey and study).
G. B. Licata.   Milan: Fratelli Treves, 1885. 334p.
Numerous Italian explorers, administrators, businessmen, missionaries and settlers have written a wide variety of works on Eritrea and Licata's account is one of the best. He also wrote *In Africa*, which was published posthumously in Florence in 1886. Other good 19th-century travel writings in the Italian language include: a brief forty-five-page account of Eritrea by an Italian official Sidney Sonnino *L'Africa Italiana: appunti di viaggio* (Italian Africa: notes on a journey), published in Rome by Tipografica della Camera dei Deputati in 1890; Eugenio Bucci di Santafiora's *A bordo della R. R. I. 'Scilla', paesaggi e tipi Africani; appunti e ricordi di una campagna idrografica lungo le coste dellacolonia Eritrea* (On board the 'Scilla', African landscape types; notes and records of a hydrographic expedition along the coast of the Eritrea colony), published in Turin by L. Roux in 1893 (260p.) which is the journal of a scientist, prefaced by Carlo de Amezaga; and Adolfo Rossi's *La nostre conquiste in Africa* (Our conquest in Africa), published in Milan by M. Kantorowicz in 1895. (97p.). The latter is an account of the author's second trip to Eritrea, particularly significant because it looks at the occupation of Agame and Italian preparations to expand into the Ethiopian interior.

21 **Africa Orientale Italiana.** (Italian East Africa).
Antonio Marra.   Rome: Editrice Nuova Europa, 1937. 213p.
In addition to Marra's description of his own travels, this book contains information on Italian colonial administration and the 1935-36 Italo-Ethiopian War, as well as a few illustrations, maps and a short bibliography.

22 **Il diario Eritreo.** (Eritrean diary).
Ferdinando Martini. Florence: Vallechi, 1947. 4 vols.

Martini was the first Italian governor of Eritrea (1898-1906) but his experience in the region began well before his term as governor. His diaries include personal and official views, descriptions, maps and illustrations. An earlier account of Martini's travels can be found in *Nell'Africa Italiana: impressioni e ricordi* (In Italian Africa: impressions and memories), published in Milan in 1891.

23 **Ost-Africanische Studien.** (East Africa Studies).
Werner von Münzinger. Schaffhausen, Germany: F. Hurter, 1864.
8 vols.

One of the most fascinating 19th-century European residents of Eritrea was Werner von Münzinger, a Swiss scholar and businessman, who settled in Keren in 1855, married an Eritrean woman and studied the language, and the social, economic and legal life of the Bilayn. He was later appointed British and French vice-consul at Massawa. An ardent protector of Catholic missions, Münzinger also worked to separate Eritrea and Tigray from Ethiopia. He was appointed governor of Massawa by the Egyptians in 1871 and later made commander of the Egyptian troops in the eastern Sudan. The above are his collected works, which were translated into Italian as *Studi sull'Africa Orientale* (Studies in East Africa) in 1890 and issued in a 584-page abridged edition by Johnson Reprint (New York, 1967). Among Münzinger's articles are some that appeared in *Zeitschrift für Allgemeine Erdkunde*: 'Die nordöstlichen Grenzländer von Habesch' (The north-eastern border of Abyssinia) (vol. 3, 1857); 'Die Schohos und die Beduan bei Massua' (The Saho and Bedouin near Massawa) (vol. 6, 1859); and 'Auszüge aus Werner Münzinger's Tagebuch, angefangen den 13 Juli 1861 bei der Abreise von Mocullu vollendet den 15 Oktober in Keren' (An extract from Werner Münzinger's journal from 13 July 1861 on the departure of Mocullu ending 15 October in Keren) (vol. 12, 1862). Von Münzinger also collaborated with T. von Heughlin and T. Kinzelbach in an article 'Die Deutsche Expedition in Ost-Afrika 1861 und 1862' (The German expedition in East Africa 1861 and 1862) (*Petermanns*, vol. 13, 1864). His later article in English 'Narrative of a journey through Afar country' (*Journal of the Royal Geographical Society*, vol. 39 [1869], p. 188-232) included some of the material above. Another German account of this period is Josef Menges' *Am Rothen Meere: Massawa* (On the Red Sea: Massawa) in *Aus Allen Weltteilen*, vol. 8 (1877), p. 182-85.

24 **Narrative of the British mission to Theodore, king of Abyssinia.**
Hormuzd Rassam. London: J. Murray, 1869. 2 vols.

This account of the 1869 British expeditionary force to Ethiopia traces the army's route from Massawa to Magdala and back to the sea. Illustrations and folded maps are included. Also related to this campaign is A. M. Honeyman's article 'Letters from Magdala and Massawa' *Bulletin of the John Rylands Library*, vol. 44 (1962).

25 **Voyage sur la côte orientale de la Mer Rouge, dans le pays d'Adal et le royaume de Choa.** (Journey to the east coast of the Red Sea, in the lands of Adal and the kingdom of Shewa).
C. E. X. Rochet d'Héricourt. Paris: A. Bertrand, 1841. 439p.

This is a French visitor's account of the Horn of Africa during the reign of Ethiopian Emperor Tewodros. A large amount of material on Eritrea is included. Rochet d'Héricourt's French-language book is accompanied by maps and illustrations. He subsequently followed this with a 409-page account, *Second voyage sur les deux rives de la Mer Rouge, dans le pays des Adels et le royaume de Choa.* (A second journey to the two coasts of the Red Sea, in the lands of the Adal and the kingdom of Shewa) published again by A. Bertrand in 1846.

26 **L'Erythrée italienne.** (Italian Eritrea).
    G. Saint-Ivens. *Bulletin de la Société de Géographie de Marseille*,
    vols. 22 (1898) and 23 (1899).

Given the proximity of the French interests in Djibouti, it is not surprising that Eritrea has seen numerous French travellers. Saint-Ivens' piece is a good example of many 19th-century accounts. Another French-language article describing travels in the 1890s is 'Notes sur l'Erythrée' (Notes on Eritrea) by L. Haneuse (*Bulletin de la Société Royale Belge Géographie*, vol. 17, 1893), which describes the author's August 1892 visit.

27 **A voyage to Abyssinia and travels into the interior of that country.**
    Henry Salt. London: F., C. & J. Rivington, 1814. 506p.

Sent by the Viscount Valentia into the Eritrean and Ethiopian highlands in 1805, Salt made a valuable record of the region at the beginning of the 1800s which includes vocabularies of local languages, maps and excellent illustrations by the author. Salt made a second journey to Eritrea in 1809-10. This work was reprinted by Frank Cass (London, 1967).

28 **Einige Mitteilungen über diesjährigen Besuch in der colonia**
    Eritrea. (Some information on this year's visit to the Eritrea colony).
    G. Schweinfurth. *Zeitschrift des Gesellschaft für Erdkunde zu Berlin*,
    vol. 19 (1892), p. 332-60.

A good summary of this prolific explorer's observations of Eritrea at the beginning of the 1890s is presented in this article. Schweinfurth's book-length account translated into Italian as *Il presente e l'avvenire della colonia Eritrea* (The present and the future of the Eritrea colony) (Milan, 1894), is extremely difficult to find outside of rare specialized collections.

29 **Voyages and travels to India, Ceylon, the Red Sea, Abyssinia and**
    Egypt in the years 1802-1806.
    Viscount Valentia. London: Miller, 1809. 286p.

George Annesley, the Viscount Valentia, provides a valuable early 19th-century account of Egypt, Eritrea, India and Sri Lanka. His connection with Henry Salt (see item no. 27) led to the compilation of a good deal of information on Eritrea. This work was also expanded and published in four volumes by F., C. & J. Rivington (London, 1811).

Ausland.
See item no. 317.

20th century

30 Eritrean journey.

Doris Burgess, Jenny Bearce, Jenny Rossiter, Trish Silkin. Trenton, New Jersey: Red Sea Press, 1985. 24p.

Eritrea and its liberation movements are described by four British women in this short illustrated travelogue, which was also a report for the British charity War on Want. A short bibliography appears on the last page.

31 Travels in Ethiopia.

David Buxton. London: Lindsay Drummond, 1949. 200p.

Buxton was a British official dispatched to Ethiopia to help combat the desert locust. His travels include the Eritrean border region, particularly the Danakil area. Buxton's account goes far beyond reporting on his own activities as he acquired both an interest and deep understanding of the region's architecture, history, culture and politics. This work is accompanied by 141 monochrome photographs. Ernest Benn published the second edition of Buxton's book in 1957.

32 Under the Red Sea sun.

Edward Ellsberg. New York: Dodd, Mead & Co., 1946. 500p.

This personal narrative of an American naval commander provides a good description of Massawa during the Second World War and contains illustrations. For an American view of the post-Second World War years, see John Gunther's *Inside Africa* (New York: Harper, 1955. 952p.) in which pages 278-81 offer a brief look at Eritrea, particularly Asmara, and discuss the American military presence and the question of Eritrea's status.

33 From Red Sea to Blue Nile: Abyssinian adventure.

Rosita Forbes. New York: Macaulay, 1925. 386p.

An excellent travelogue, this offers a good view of Eritrea and Ethiopia in the period before the 1935 Italian invasion of Ethiopia. This edition includes fifty-nine excellent illustrations and a folding map. It was also published in London by Cassell in 1925 with sixty-one illustrations.

34 Mer Rouge. (Red Sea).

Gaetan Fouquet. Paris: J. Susse, 1946. 196p.

This French-language work on the Red Sea includes fifty photographs.

35 Ethiopian journeys: travels in Ethiopia 1969-72.

Paul Henze. London: Ernest Benn, 1977. 287p.

Numerous illustrations and maps are included in this account by a United States Embassy official, currently a consultant on the Horn of Africa. Henze's travels encompass Eritrea, as well as Ethiopia, and his account is sympathetic and detailed. A bibliography appears on pages 275-76.

36 **African calliope.**
Edward Hoagland. Harmondsworth, England: Penguin, 1981. 272p.
Primarily a travelogue of the author's journey to the Sudan, this well-written book
includes an excellent chapter on Eritrea (Chapter eight). The revised edition (1995)
contains a new postscript.

37 **Le drame éthiopien.** (The Ethiopian drama).
Henry de Monfreid. Paris: Editions Bernard Grasset, 1935. 243p.
This French-language book is an account of the author's travels in Eritrea and
Ethiopia in 1933-34. In spite of the title, the majority of this fascinating travelogue
deals with Eritrea under the Italians, with much space devoted to Massawa, Asmara,
the Dahlak Archipelago and colonial concerns. Fifty-eight interesting photographs are
included.

38 **Pearls, arms and hashish: pages from the life of a Red Sea
navigator.**
Henry de Monfreid. London: Victor Gollancz, 1930. 349p.
De Monfreid's memoirs as a ship's captain and adventurer in the Red Sea are
collected here by Ida Treat. Massawa was one of his frequent ports of call and his
knowledge of Eritrea and the legitimate and illicit trading patterns of the Horn of
Africa is considerable. His other English-language works include *Secrets of the Red
Sea* (translated by Helen Buchanan Bell. London: Faber & Faber, 1934. 317p.),
Hashish (translated by Helen Buchanan Bell. London: MacDonald, 1974. 284p.) and
the now rare *Sea adventures*.

39 **Colonial postscript: diary of a district officer.**
John Morley. London: Radcliffe Press, 1992. 212p.
This is a collection of the memoirs of a British administrator posted to Eritrea during
the period of British occupation (1941-52). Also included are eight pages of plates
and portraits by Patricia Morley.

40 **Avventura in Africa Orientale Italiana.** (Adventure in Italian East
Africa).
Brana Nelusky. Naples: Tipomeccanica, 1968. 252p.
Nelusky's account is most notable for its good illustrations.

41 **Ethiopian adventure: from the Red Sea to the Blue Nile.**
Herbert Rittlinger. London: Oldhams Press, 1959. 224p.
Translated from the German by Eva Wilson, Rittlinger's description of his journey
includes much on the Eritrean coast and highlands. Illustrations are contained in the
text.

Geography

42   **Risultati scientifici di un viaggio nella colonia Eritrea.** (Scientific
results of a journey in Eritrea colony).
Giotto Dainelli, Olinto Marinelli.   Florence: Galetti e Cocci, 1912.
601p.
Dainelli and Marinelli gathered and recorded a great deal of information on the
geography, geology, topography, climate, local housing and culture of Eritrea,
especially of the Afar. This valuable work contains numerous diagrams and
photographs.

43   **L'Abissinia e le colonia Italiana sul Mar Rosso.** (Abyssinia and the
Italian colony in the Red Sea).
Francesco Fasolo.   Caserta, Italy: A. Iaselli, 1887.
This work offers a general overview of the geography of the Horn of Africa, and is
particularly good on the topography of Massawa and its vicinity. A valuable early
map of Massawa and its surrounding area accompany this work.

44   **La Mer Rouge: l'Abyssinie et l'Arabie aux XVIe et XVIIe siècles et
la cartographie des portulans du monde orientale.** (The Red Sea:
Abyssinia and Arabia in the 16th and 17th centuries and the Portuguese
cartography of the eastern world).
Albert Kammerer.   Cairo: Société Royale de Géographie d'Egypte,
1947-52. 3 vols. bibliog.
This French-language geographical reference work was compiled from Portuguese
accounts and pilot guides of the Red Sea region, particularly Eritrea and the Arabian
peninsula. It contains numerous maps, charts, illustrations and quotes, all of which
will be of interest to modern geographers and historians. This work is introduced by
G. Hanotaux and an extensive bibliography appears at the beginning of the first
volume.

12

45 **An introductory geography of Ethiopia.**
Mesfin Wolde-Mariam. Addis Ababa: Haile Selassie University Press, 1972. 215p.

Few general geographies have been written specifically on Eritrea and none of them are recent. This text was written for first-year students at an Ethiopian university and is adequate for an introductory knowledge of Eritrean geography. Maps and illustrations are included. Two good general geographical articles in English are 'Ethiopia, Eritrea and Somalia' by J. Haggag and R. J. Harrison Church (*Geographical Review*, vol. 43, 1953); and 'A question of time' by Richard Evans (*Geographical Magazine*, vol. 63, no. 8 [August 1991], p. 22-25).

Birth of a nation.
See item no. 1.

East African handbook.
See item no. 4.

The Blue Nile.
See item no. 81.

The Ethiopians.
See item no. 113.

The Ethiopia Observer.
See item no. 305.

The Environment and Climate

46 **An African winter.**
Preston King.   Harmondsworth, England: Penguin, 1986. 249p.
The effects of drought, war, aid and famine on the environment and peoples of Africa are the principal topics of this work. Particularly good are analyses of the famine in the Horn of Africa and the effects of war in Eritrea.

47 **Starting from scratch: the greening of Eritrea.**
Julia Rossetti.   *Ceres*, vol. 25, no. 6 (November/December 1993), p. 4-6.
This article describes a 1993 environmental restoration programme in which some 200,000 Eritreans planted several million trees, mainly leucaena and eucalyptus.

48 **Africa in crisis.**
Lloyd Timberlake.   London: Earthscan, 1985. 232p.
Subtitled 'the causes, the cures of environmental bankruptcy', this book deals with Africa's principal environmental difficulties. Subjects covered include famine, poverty, population, health, misuse of resources, forests, energy, soil, crops, fisheries, Apartheid, conflict, aid and development. A great deal of the material in Timberlake's work applies to Eritrea, which features prominently several times.

East African handbook.
See item no. 4.

Risultati scientifici di un viaggio nella colonia Eritrea. (Scientific results of a journey in Eritrea colony).
See item no. 42.

Red Sea.
See item no. 57.

Geology and Oceanography

49   **Rifting or drifting in the Red Sea.**
Enrico Bonatti.   *Nature* (24 December 1987), p. 692-93.

Bonatti attempts to separate geology from mythology in this analysis of the tectonic movements under and around the Red Sea. A controversy has long raged over the exact nature of the region's tectonics. To continue this scientific debate, see William Bosworth's 'The nature of the Red Sea crust: a controversy revisited' (*Geology*, vol. 21, no. 6 [June 1993], p. 574-76). 'Accretion tectonics in Northern Eritrea revealed by remotely sensed imagery' by S. A. Drury and S. M. Berhe (*Geological Magazine*, vol. 130, no. 2 [March 1993], p. 177-90) and 'Structures related to Red Sea evolution in Northern Eritrea' by S. A. Drury, S. P. Kelley and M. Abraha (*Tectonics*, vol. 13, no. 6 [December 1994], p. 1,371) are two articles examining geological faults in Eritrea in the light of newly gathered data. On the basis of this information, the country has been divided into three distinct geological zones: the Hagar; the Nacfa (Nak'fa); and the Barka.

50   **The geologic evolution of the Red Sea.**
Robert G. Coleman.   Oxford: Clarendon Press, 1993. 186p. bibliog.

This comprehensive examination of a controversial topic is part of the series Oxford Monographs on Geology and Geophysics (no. 24). A bibliography appears on pages 153-74.

51   **Hot brines and recent heavy metal deposits in the Red Sea: a geochemical and geophysical account.**
Egon T. Degens, David A. Ross.   New York: Springer-Verlag, 1969. 600p. bibliog.

Metal ore deposits under the Red Sea are explored in this detailed, scientific study which contains good illustrations and bibliographical references. Most studies on Red Sea deposits are related to Egypt, the Sudan and Saudi Arabia. However, there is much evidence to suggest that Eritrean waters cover a seabed with numerous resources.

52 **The blue continent.**
Folco Quilici, Giorgio Ravelli.   New York: Rinehart, 1954. 246p.
This illustrated account of marine life and deep-sea diving in the Red Sea was the
result of the 1952-53 Italian National Underwater Expedition.

53 **Dahlak: with the Italian National Underwater Expedition in the
Red Sea.**
Gianni Roghi, Francesco Baschieri, edited by Eleanor Brockett,
translated from the Italian by Priscilla Hastings.   London: N. Kaye,
1956. 280p.
This account of an Italian expedition examines the marine biology and deep-sea
diving conditions around the Dahlak archipelago, an Eritrean coral island group just
east of Massawa.

54 **Notizie idrografiche sull'Africa Orientale Italiana.** (Hydrographic
notes on Italian East Africa).
Anonymous.   Rome: Istituto Poligrafico dello Stato, 1936. 77p.
The rivers, water supply and drainage patterns of Eritrea, Ethiopia and Somalia are
surveyed in this good early work with tables, diagrams and two folding maps.

Risultati scientifici di un viaggio nella colonia Eritrea. (Scientific results
of a journey in Eritrea colony).
See item no. 42.

Fauna of the Red Sea.
See item no. 55.

Manta: under the Red Sea with spear and camera.
See item no. 59.

**Spawning and development of three coral-associated Lithophaga species
in the Red Sea.**
See item no. 60.

Studies on crustacea of the Red Sea.
See item no. 61.

The manzanar, mullet, milkfish and mosquite project in Eritrea.
See item no. 62.

**Red Sea, Gulf of Aden and Suez Canal: a bibliography on
oceanographic and marine environmental research.**
See item no. 338.

**Bibliografia geologica Italiana per gli anni 1915-1933: Africa Orientale
Italiana.** (Italian geological bibliography for the years 1915-1933: Italian
East Africa).
See item no. 341.

Flora and Fauna

55 **Fauna of the Red Sea.**
C. Amirithalingam. Khartoum: University of Khartoum Press, 1970.
113p. bibliog.
This contribution to the marine biology of the Red Sea can be applied to the study of Eritrean waters. It contains a bibliography on pages 96-104. See also: *Fishes of the genus eviota of the Red Sea with descriptions of three new species (teleostei gobiidae)* by Ernest A. Lachner and Susan J. Karnelia (Washington DC: Smithsonian Institution Press, 1978. 23p.).

56 **Preliminary data on the Anopheles gambiae complex (diptera: Culicidae) in some sites in western Eritrea.**
G. Carrara. *Parassitologia*, supplement to vol. 36 (June 1994), p. 30.
This authoritative work on malaria-bearing mosquitoes is the result of the eighteenth national congress of the Societa Italiana di Parassitologia (Italian Parasitology Society), held in June 1994.

57 **Red Sea.**
Alasdair J. Edwards, Stephen M. Head. Oxford: Pergamon Press, 1987. 441p.
Published in collaboration with the International Union for Conservation of Nature and Natural Resources, this well-researched book examines the Red Sea environment and its preservation. The foreword is written by the Duke of Edinburgh and a good bibliography is included.

58 **The birds of North Africa from the Canary Islands to the Red Sea.**
Robert Daniel Etchecopar, François Hue. Edinburgh: Oliver & Boyd, 1967. 612p. maps.
Translated from the French by P. A. D. Hollom, this guide to the birds of North Africa is also useful for Eritrea. Maps and illustrations by Paul Barruel are excellent.

59 **Manta: under the Red Sea with spear and camera.**
Hans Hass, translated from the German by James Cleugh. New York: Rand McNally, 1953. 278p.

This illustrated work describes the underwater photography of Red Sea fishes and other marine fauna. Eighty-one photographs and two maps are contained in this excellent book. Cruising and sport fishing in the Red Sea is covered in 'A time of fish' by George Day (*Cruising World*, vol. 19, no. 11 [November 1993], p. 17-18). An interesting illustrated book on sharks is *Shark cage under the Red Sea* by Ted Falcon-Barker (Philadelphia: Chilton, 1969. 114p.).

60 **Spawning and development of three coral-associated Lithophaga species in the Red Sea.**
O. Modaky. *Marine Biology*, vol. 115, no. 2 (1993), p. 245-52.

A recent study of the reproduction of Red Sea mussels in Eritrean waters.

61 **Studies on crustacea of the Red Sea.**
Otton Michailovich Paulson. Jerusalem: Israel Program for Scientific Translations, 1961. 164p.

This excellent early work on crustaceans is useful for the study of both marine biology and the fishing industry. Translated by Francis D. Por, Paulson's illustrated work was originally published in Kiev in 1875. It was also issued in its English translation by the Office of Technical Services of the United States Department of Commerce.

62 **The manzanar, mullet, milkfish and mosquite project in Eritrea.**
G. H. Sato. *Annals of Clinical Biochemistry*, vol. 5 (September 1992), p. 88.

A recent contribution to the study of the fishes in Eritrean coastal waters.

63 **Beitrag zur Flora Aethiopiens.** (A contribution to Ethiopian flora).
G. A. Schweinfurth. Berlin: G. Reimer, 1867. 311p.

Eritrea's botany is well covered in this early work by the renowned German explorer Schweinfurth.

64 **A field guide to the butterflies of Africa.**
John George Williams. London: Collins, 1971. 238p.

A number of the butterflies in this guide can be found in Eritrea. Williams' comprehensive guide includes colour plates, illustrations and a short bibliography.

65 **A field guide to the birds of East Africa.**
John George Williams. London: Collins, 1980. 288p.

Eritrea is either the habitat of, or lies on the migration routes of, a large number of the birds in this excellent guide, which contains colour plates, illustrations and a short bibliography.

66   **A plague of locusts.**
      Anonymous.   *The New Scientist*, vol. 137, no. 1,857 (23 January
      1993), p. 11.
This news item examines the possibility of desert locust outbreaks which would
damage the economy of Eritrea and other countries on the coasts of the southern Red
Sea.

The blue continent.
See item no. 52.

**Dahlak: with the Italian National Underwater Expedition in the Red
Sea.**
See item no. 53.

Prehistory and Archaeology

67 **Première campagne de fouilles à Matara.** (The first excavation
season at Matara).
Francis Anfray. *Annales d'Ethiopie*, vol. 5 (1963), p. 87-166.

This lengthy article is the first account of the excavation of the Eritrean highland
urban site of Matara in 1959, when a large building of the Aksumite era was cleared.
Numerous photographs and diagrams accompany this work. Subsequent work on this
site can be found in: Anfray's paper with Guy Annequin 'Matara: deuxième,
troisième et quatrième campagnes de fouilles' (Matara: second, third and fourth
excavation seasons) in *Annales d'Ethiopie* (vol. 6 [1965], p. 49-87); Roger
Schneider's 'Notes épigraphiques sur les découvertes de Matara' (Epigraphic notes
on the Matara finds) in *Annales d'Ethiopie* (vol. 6 [1965], p. 88-92); Anfray's
'Matara' in *Annales d'Ethiopie* (vol. 7 [1967], p. 33-88); and Anfray's 'Deux villes
axoumites: Adoulis et Matara' (Two Aksumite towns: Adulis and Matara) which is on
pages 745-65 in *VI Congresso Internazionale di Studi Etiopici* (*Roma 1972*)
published in Rome by Accademia Nazionale dei Lincei in 1974.

68 **Notes archéologiques.** (Archaeological notes).
Francis Anfray. *Annales d'Ethiopie*, vol. 8 (1970), p. 31-42.

Information on archaeological finds in Eritrea is provided in this illustrated French-
language article. For up-dated material, see 'Archaeology in Northern Ethiopia' by
Kathryn A. Bard (*Context*, vol. 10, no. 4 [1992-93], p. 20-22).

69 **Temple d'Appolon Daphnephoros.** (The Temple of Apollo
Daphnephoros).
Paul Auberson.   Bern: Editions Francke, 1968. 24p.

This brief work on an ancient temple in Eritrea contains nine maps and diagrams in
pockets.

70   **Prehistoric cultures of the Horn of Africa.**
John Desmond Clark.   Cambridge, England: Cambridge University
Press, 1954. 385p. bibliog.
Sponsored by Cambridge University's Museum of Archaeology and Ethnology, this
work is a good starting point for scholarship on the archaeology of Eritrea. It is
accompanied by illustrations, a folding map and a bibliography (p. 369-74). A good
article to up-date Clark's material is 'Cultural beginning: Plio-Pleistocene
archaeological occurrences from the Afar' by John W. K. Harris (*African
Archaeological Review*, vol. 1, no. 1. [January 1983], p. 3-31).

71   **Deutsche Aksum-Expedition.** (German Aksum expedition).
Edited by Enno Littmann.   Berlin: Georg Reimer, 1913. 4 vols.
Well produced and thorough, this record of the 1906 German archaeological
expedition to Ethiopia remains a classic work. The destination of the team was
Aksum, the Tigrayan city south of the Eritrean border. However, these journals also
record much that is of interest between Aksum and the Eritrean coast. Many
photographs, maps and other illustrations are included. Littmann went on to lead
Princeton University's expeditions to the region and subsequently edited *Publications
of the Princeton Expedition to Abyssinia*, a four-volume record (Leiden: Brill,
1910-15).

72   **British Museum excavations at Adulis.**
Stuart Munro-Hay.   *Antiquaries Journal*, vol. 39, no. 1 (January
1989), p. 43-52.
Adulis, the chief seaport on the ancient Eritrean coast, has seen the uncovering of a
number of buildings and the discovery of quantities of coins, pottery and other
artifacts. There is still a lot to be discovered about this site which has seen some
unparalleled finds. Munro-Hay provides a look at some early archaeological work in
the area. The most important early archaeologist to excavate in Adulis was the Italian,
Roberto Paribeni, who wrote 'Ricercha nel Luogo dell'Antica Adulis' (Research on
the site of ancient Adulis) in *Rendiconti dei Accademia dei Lincei* in 1908.

73   **The Ona sites of Asmara and Hamasien.**
Stuart Munro-Hay, Giuseppe Tringali.   *Rassegna di Studi Etiopici*,
vol. 35 (1991), p. 135-70.
This article offers an account of survey work and excavations of ruins in Eritrea
which explores possible links with discoveries made by Rodolfo Fattovich in the
Gash Delta. Tringali also published several articles on archaeological work in Eritrea,
including: 'Cenni sulle Ona di Asmara e dintorni' (Notes on the Ona of Asmara and
its surroundings) in *Annales d'Ethiopie* (vol. 6 [1965], p. 143-61); 'Necropoli di
Curbacaiehat (Asmara)' (Necropolis of Curbacaiehat [Asmara]), *Journal of Ethiopian
Studies* (vol. 5 [1967], p. 109); 'Necropoli de Cascassé e oggetti Sudarabici dalla
regione di Asmara' (Necropolis of Kaskase and South Arabian objects from the
Asmara region), *Rassegna di Studi Etiopici* (vol. 26 [1978], p. 47-66); 'Note su
ritrovamenti archeologici in Eritrea' (Note on archaeological discoveries in Eritrea),
Rassegna di Studi Etiopici (vol. 28 [1980-81], p. 99-113); and 'Varietà di asce litiche
in Ouna dell'altipiaad Eritreo' (Types of stone axes in ona of the Ethiopian plateau),
Journal of Ethiopian Studies (vol. 7 [1969], p. 119).

74   **Una civilta scomparsa dell'Eritrea e gli scavi archeologici nella regione di Cheren.** (A vanished civilization of Eritrea and archaeological excavations in the Keren region).
Abele Piva.   *Nuova Antologia* (1907), p. 323-35.

At Aratu, near Keren, an Aksumite building was uncovered, which suggests that the Aksumite empire reached quite far north. The exact boundaries of the empire have yet to be determined.

Azania.
See item no. 318.

Paideuma.
See item no. 330.

Proceedings of the Third International Conference on Ethiopian Studies.
See item no. 331.

History

Histories of Africa and the Horn of Africa

75 **Freebooters of the Red Sea: pirates, politicians and pieces of eight.**
Hamilton Cochran. Indianapolis, Indiana: Bobbs-Merrill, 1965. 223p.
Constitutes an examination of piracy in the Red Sea with illustrations and maps. A short bibliography also appears on pages 216-18.

76 **Italy in Africa.**
M. Christopher Hollis. London: Hamish Hamilton , 1941. 253p.
This is a British view of Italian colonialism in Eritrea, Somalia, Libya and Ethiopia. Another good introduction to Italian colonial schemes is Patricia Wright's article 'Italy's African Dream' (*History Today*, vol. 23, nos. 4 and 5 [April and May 1973]).

77 **La missione dell'Italia in Africa.** (Italy's mission in Africa).
Alessandro Lessona. Rome: Istituto Nazionale Facista di Cultura, 1936. 88p.
A Fascist argument for the Italian annexation of Ethiopia is presented in this short booklet. Lessona wrote a similar monograph on the African debates in the Italian Chamber of Deputies, *L'Africa Italiana nel primo anno dell'Impero* (Italian Africa one year after empire) (Rome: Istituto Poligrafico dello Stato, 1937. 47p.).

78 **The Italo-Abyssinian war, the operations: Massawa-Addis Ababa.**
H. P. Lloyd. *R.A.F. Quarterly*, vol. 8 (1937), p. 357-67.
Lloyd's article provides a good description of Italian military operations in 1935-36. For a continuation of the military narrative, see 'The fall of Mussolini's East African empire' by P. Lessing in *The history of the Second World War*, part 14 (1973), p. 365-73.

79   **L'impérialisme colonial italien de 1870 à nos jours.** (Italian colonial imperialism from 1870 to the present day).
J. L. Miège.   Paris: Société d'Edition d'Enseignement Superieur, 1968. 419p.

This is an excellent French-language introduction to the history of Italian colonialism in Eritrea, Somalia and Ethiopia between 1870 and 1941. Good maps and an extensive bibliography (pages 285 to 308) add to this book's many merits.

80   **L'Italia in Africa.** (Italy in Africa).
Edited by Elio Migliorini.   Rome: Istituto Poligrafico dello Stato, 1955. 2 vols. bibliog.

Well researched and thorough, Migliorini's massive work on the Italian colonies in Africa includes ethnographical, political, economic and social information, travellers' accounts, documentary material, tables, maps, statistics and bibliographical references.

81   **The Blue Nile.**
Alan Moorehead.   London: Hamish Hamilton, 1962. 308p. bibliog.

A vivid overview of events in the Horn of Africa from the early 1700s to 1869, Moorehead's book has appeared in several editions, including a 1983 illustrated edition published by Vintage. The region's geography and the historical eras before and after the principal period covered are summarized and a bibliography is provided on pages 291-95.

82   **Africa Orientale Italiana: cinquanta anni dopo.** (Italian East Africa: fifty years later).
Pier Francesco Nistri.   Rome: Wage, 1990. 109p. bibliog.

This short work contains memoirs of and reflections on the Italian occupation of Ethiopia. A short bibliography is included.

83   **The scramble for Africa.**
Thomas Pakenham.   New York: Random House, 1991. 738p. bibliog.

An excellent book, this traces the colonization of the African continent from 1876 to 1912. Although it tends to emphasize British imperialism, the activities of the Italians are also presented. Chapter twenty-six deals with the establishment of the Italian colony of Eritrea and Italy's disastrous attempt to conquer Ethiopia at the end of the 19th century. This book is meant to show the European motives, activities and conditions which led to the division of Africa among the colonial powers. As such, it is a very readable, accurate, well-documented and uniquely comprehensive account. Included are a chronology, fifty-one photographs, numerous other illustrations and maps and a good bibliography.

84   **L'Africa Italiana.** (Italian Africa).
Augusto Pierantoni.   Rome: Officina Poligrafica Editrice, 1908. 307p.

Pierantoni's Italian-language volume considers the state of Eritrea at the turn of the century. It was intended to be the first of a series but no further volumes were published. A much shorter treatment of this era in English is 'Italian colonial expansion: its origins, progress and difficulties' by A. Baldacci (*United Empire*, vol. 2, 1911). The period immediately following the First World War is covered in the rare *L'Africa Orientale Italiana e i suoi precedenti storici* (Italian East Africa and its historical precedents) by Cesare Cesari (Rome, 1926)

85 **Diario Africana orientale Italiana.** (Italian East African diary).
Ciro Poggiali.   Milan: Longanesi, 1971. 297p.
Poggiali's personal narrative of the Italo-Ethiopian War extends from 15 June 1936 to 4 October 1937 during which time he was a correspondent for *Corriere della Sera*. Described as 'secret notes', it contains much which was not reported at the time. Well illustrated, this work is accompanied by twenty-two plates.

86 **Storia e politica coloniale Italiana: 1869-1937.** (Italian colonial history and politics: 1869-1937).
Renzo Sertoli Salis.   Messina: G. Principato, 1938. 346p.
Written by a legal scholar who was part of the Italian occupation authorities in Ethiopia, this history strongly emphasizes Eritrea and Italian nationalism. Sertoli Salis also wrote on the causes, diplomacy and international legal issues behind the Italo-Ethiopian War of 1935-36 in *Il conflitto Italo-Etiopico e la Societa delle nazioni* (The Italo-Ethiopian conflict and the League of Nations) (Milan: G. Martucci, 1936).

87 **Suakin and Massawa under Egyptian rule: 1865-1885.**
Ghada H. Talhami.   Washington DC: University Press of America, 1979. 309p. bibliog.
This well-researched, specialized work details the two most significant decades of Egyptian colonialism along the Red Sea. An excellent bibliography is added on pages 291-305.

88 **Africa Orientale Italiana.** (Italian East Africa).
Giovanni Vaccaro.   Milan: Marescalchi, 1936. 206p.
Sub-titled 'a book on the heroism and glory', this illustrated Italian-language account of Eritrea, Ethiopia and Somalia constitutes a highly nationalistic description of events in the 1930s. A similar Italian-language book of this era is *L'Africa Orientale Italiana e l'Abissinia* (Italian East Africa and Abyssinia) by Nicola Malizia (Naples: Chiurazzi, 1935. 270p.).

The Prester John of the Indies.
See item no. 7.

Travels to discover the sources of the Nile in the years 1768-1773.
See item no. 9.

The Red Sea and adjacent countries.
See item no. 12.

A voyage to Abyssinia.
See item no. 14.

Travellers in Ethiopia.
See item no. 15.

Travels of the Jesuits in Ethiopia.
See item no. 17.

The Portuguese expedition to Abyssinia in 1541-53, as narrated by Castanhoso.
See item no. 18.

A journey through Abyssinia.
See item no. 19.

From Red Sea to Blue Nile: Abyssinian adventure.
See item no. 33.

Avventura in Africa Orientale Italiana. (Adventure in Italian East Africa).
See item no. 40.

Christentum am Rotem Meer. (Christianity on the Red Sea).
See item no. 163.

The Church of Ethiopia: a panorama of history and spiritual life.
See item no. 164.

The Ethiopia Observer.
See item no. 305.

A historical dictionary of Ethiopia and Eritrea.
See item no. 324.

Journal of African History.
See item no. 326.

Journal of Ethiopian Studies.
See item no. 328.

Proceedings of the Fifth International Conference on Ethiopian Studies.
See item no. 332.

Histories of Ethiopia

Ancient and mediaeval

89   **Ethiopia and the Red Sea: the rise and decline of the Solomonic dynasty and Muslim-European rivalry in the region.**
Mordechai Abir.   London: Frank Cass, 1980. 251p.

A valuable overview of the Horn of Africa before the Italian colonial era is provided by Abir in this work. He also includes a good bibliography and a number of maps.

90 **The Ethiopian slave trade and its relation to the Islamic world.**
Mordechai Abir. In: *Slaves and slavery in Muslim Africa.* Edited by
John Ralph Willis. London: F. Cass, 1985. p. 123-37.
Abir's analysis of the Ethiopia-Arabia slave trade is found in volume one of this two-volume work, which is divided into 'Islam and the ideology of enslavement' and 'The servile estate'. Bibliographical sources are included for each section.

91 **The Ethiopian in Greek and Roman civilization.**
Grace Hadley Beardsley. Baltimore, Maryland: Johns Hopkins
University Press, 1922. 145p.
Ethiopian connections with the ancient Mediterranean world are explored in this work which concentrates on history, art and archaeology. The first three chapters consist of the author's revised PhD thesis.

92 **India and Ethiopia from the seventh century B. C.**
Sunti Kumar Chatterji. Calcutta: Asiatic Society, 1968. 80p. (Asiatic
Society monography, no. 15).
This is a good, short paper on the early trade and other ties between Ethiopia and India, largely conducted through the ancient Eritrean port of Adulis, near present-day Massawa.

93 **Antiquities of north Ethiopia.**
Otto A. Jager. Stuttgart: Brockhaus, 1965. 164p. bibliog.
Archaeological and historical findings in Eritrea and Tigray are described in detail in Jager's book. The second (1974) edition of this work was produced in collaboration with Ivy Pearce and was simultaneously published in London by Paul, Trench, Trubner & Co. Among this book's good illustrations are maps and eight leaves of plates. A bibliography appears on pages 157 to 162.

94 **Axum.**
Yuri M. Kobishchanov, translated from the Russian by Lorraine T.
Kapitanoff. University Park, Pennsylvania: Pennsylvania State
University, 1979. 348p. bibliog.
The territory of present-day Eritrea formed the Red Sea coastal provinces, and hence the main trading centre, of the ancient Aksumite (Axumite) Empire. This excellent illustrated work on Aksum provides a rare general history and contains a good bibliography on pages 315-34. For an article on early Aksum and the story of its origins, see 'The legend of the Queen of Sheba in the tradition of Axum' by Enno Littman (*Biblioteca Abessinica*, vol. 1 [Leiden], 1904). For an acount of Christianity in Aksum, *The conversion experience in Axum during the fourth and fifth centuries* by Clifton Brown (Washington DC: Howard University Press, 1973) is of value. A good French-language reference and chronology on the kings of Aksum is *Les listes des rois d'Aksoum* (Lists of the Aksumite kings) by Carlo Conti-Rossini (*Journal Asiatique*, vol. 10, no. 14 [1909], p. 263-320).

The Suma oriental of Tome Pires.
See item no. 10.

The Periplus of the Erythraean Sea.
See item no. 16.

Première campagne de fouilles à Matara. (The first excavation season at Matara).
See item no. 67.

Notes archéologiques. (Archaeological notes).
See item no. 68.

Temple d'Appolon Daphnephoros. (The Temple of Apollo Daphnephoros).
See item no. 69.

Deutsche Aksum-Expedition. (German Aksum Expedition).
See item no. 71.

British Museum excavations at Adulis.
See item no. 72.

The Ona sites of Asmara and Hamasien.
See item no. 73.

Una civilta scomparsa dell'Eritrea e gli scavi archeologici nella regione di Cheren. (A vanished civilization of Eritrea and archaeological excavations in the Keren region).
See item no. 74.

The church history of Ethiopia.
See item no. 165.

Lo stato etiopico e la sua chiesa. (The Ethiopian state and its church).
See item no. 168.

La necropoli islamica di Dahlak Kebir nei Mar Rossi. (The Islamic necropolis on Grand Dahlak in the Red Sea).
See item no. 173.

Abba Salama.
See item no. 313.

Modern

95 **La guerra d'Etiopia.** (The war in Ethiopia).
Pietro Badoglio. Milan: A. Mondadori, 1936. 249p.

An official Italian view of the 1935 invasion of Ethiopia is provided by Marshal Badoglio, the rash commander of the Italian forces attacking from Eritrea. The preface is written by Benito Mussolini. Both Badoglio and Mussolini were eager to justify the invasion and to minimize the difficulties faced by their forces. Although this work was translated from the Italian as *The war in Abyssinia* (London, 1940), the original is more easily available.

96 **The coming of the Italian-Ethiopian war.**
George W. Baer. Cambridge, Massachusetts: Harvard University
Press, 1967. 404p. bibliog.
This American analysis of the background to the Italian invasion of Ethiopia is largely based on sources from Italian archives. Containing a twenty-two-page bibliography, it includes a large amount of material on Eritrea as an Italian base. Also of use on the period before the Italian invasion is *The Wal Wal arbitration* by Pitman B. Potter (Washington DC: Carnegie Endowment for International Peace, 1938. 182p.). This important book describes the incident which sparked off the controversy between Italy and Ethiopia, and which eventually led Mussolini to invade Ethiopia in 1935.

97 **The civilizing mission: a history of the Italo-Ethiopian war of 1935-1936.**
A. J. Barker. New York: Dial Press, 1968. 383p. bibliog.
Barker provides a good examination of the brutal invasion of Ethiopia by Italy. Eritrea's role is noted in detail. Illustrations, maps and a good bibliography (pages 355-67) are included. A similar work is Thomas M. Coffey's *Lion by the tail: the story of the Italian-Ethiopian war* (New York: Viking Press, 1974. 369p.).

98 **The question of the union of churches in Luso-Ethiopian relations: 1500-1632.**
Girma Beshah, Merid Wolde Aregay. Lisbon: Junta de Investigacoes
de Ultramar and Centro de Estudos Historicos Ultramarinos, 1964.
115p. bibliog.
In the early 16th century the Portuguese were welcomed as saviours by the Christians of the Eritrean and Ethiopian highlands. However, within a century and a quarter, Lisbon's envoys, soldiers and missionaries would be expelled as undesirables. Portuguese relations with the rulers and peoples of the Horn of Africa are explored in this short book, which also deals in detail with the conflict between Catholicism and Orthodoxy. A five-page bibliography and genealogical tables are provided.

99 **The lost empire: the story of the Jesuits in Ethiopia, 1555-1634.**
Philip Caraman. Notre Dame, Indiana: University of Notre Dame
Press, 1985. 176p. maps.
The heavy-handed tactics of Portuguese Jesuit missionaries brought about their expulsion from the Ethiopian Empire and the Eritrean coast in 1634. This history of the 79-year period of Portuguese influence in the Horn of Africa is very readable and contains good photographs and maps.

100 **Black shirt, black skin.**
Boake Carter. London: George Allen & Unwin; Harrisburg,
Pennsylvania: Telegraph Press, 1935. 178p.
Carter's report deals with the causes of the Italo-Ethiopian conflict, with American relations with Ethiopia and with slavery in that country. The book is illustrated by George P. Fayko and contains a map on its lining paper. Another American account of this era is '"Ethiopia, here I come" says Mussolini' by G. D. Blomgren, published

in Waterloo, Iowa in 1936. More specific to Eritrea is H. P. Lechenberg's 'With the Italians in Eritrea' (*National Geographic Magazine*, vol. 68, no. 3 [September 1935], p. 265-95).

101   **The Ethiopian War 1935-1941.**
Translated by P. D. Cummins.   Chicago: University of Chicago Press, 1969. 289p. maps.
This collection of translated Italian documents and accounts is a valuable work for anyone studying the Italo-Ethiopian War of 1935-36 and the fall of Eritrea to British forces in 1941. The volume contains a number of good maps.

102   **Red tears: war, famine and revolution in Ethiopia.**
Dawit Wolde Giorgis.   Trenton, New Jersey: Red Sea Press, 1989. 375p.
A former member of the Central Committee of the Ethiopian Communist Party and head of the Ethiopian Relief and Recovery Administration, Dawit Wolde Giorgis presents the interesting viewpoint of an insider who flees and becomes a critic of the Ethiopian Revolution. Eritrea plays a key role throughout his book, which covers the period from 1974 to 1988.

103   **Anno XIII: the conquest of an empire.**
Emilio de Bono.   London: Cresset Press, 1937. 314p. maps.
De Bono was the first commander of Italian troops in Eritrea at the start of the 1935 invasion of Ethiopia. Cautious and careful, he was replaced with Badoglio by Mussolini, who wrote the introduction to this book. De Bono's account is illustrated and contains several maps. The translation of this work is unattributed.

104   **The invention of Ethiopia.**
Bonnie K. Holcomb, Sisai Ibssa.   Trenton, New Jersey: Red Sea Press, 1990. 450p. bibliog.
Sub-titled 'the making of a dependent colonial state in northeast Africa', Holcomb and Ibssa's work argues the leftist position that Ethiopia is not a naturally occurring political, cultural or economic entity, but rather a European colonial invention. The authors see this 'unnatural' state of affairs as being responsible for the region's instability and use many Eritrean and Oromo examples to illustrate their argument. There is a good glossary (in the front of the book) and a bibliography.

105   **A history of Abyssinia.**
A. H. M. Jones, E. Monroe.   Oxford: Clarendon Press, 1935. 188p.
The Aksumite period and Italian colonial era in Eritrea receive a good overview in this work which was published at a time when world attention was focused on the Italian invasion of Ethiopia. A folding map is included.

106   **A new history of Ethiopia.**
Job Ludolph.   London: S. Smith, 1684. various paginations.
This outstanding 17th-century study includes much material on Eritrea, mainly gleaned from other travellers' accounts.

107 **A history of Ethiopia.**
Harold G. Marcus. Berkeley, California: University of California Press, 1994. 261p. bibliog. maps.

A controversial view presented by Marcus defines Ethiopia as a 'greater' Ethiopia which includes Eritrea and which unifies and divides throughout history. Maps, a good bibliography and a useful glossary are provided.

108 **History of the Abyssinia expedition.**
Clements R. Markham. London: Macmillan, 1869. 484p.

Markham's history is a contemporary account of the British military expedition to Ethiopia in 1867-68. This force was sent, via the Eritrean coast, to free European hostages held by the Ethiopian Emperor Tewodros. Illustrations include seven leaves of plates. Markham's book, which provides a good detailed description of Eritrea in the mid-19th century, was reprinted in 1970 by Gregg International Publishers of Westmead, England. Also related to Eritrean history is Markham's article 'The Portuguese expeditions to Abysinnia in the fifteenth, sixteenth and seventeenth centuries' (*Journal of the Royal Geographical Society*, vol. 38 [1869], p. 4-12).

109 **Italy's conflict with Ethiopia: the facts of the case.**
Augusto Rosso. New York: The American League for Italy, 1935. 14p.

Italy's case against Ethiopia was pressed forward by Italian interest groups and ethnic associations. Dr Rosso's address was delivered at a dinner of the Order of the Sons of Italy (an Italian-American organization) in Boston on 14 October 1935, within a day of Ethiopia's invasion by Italian forces.

110 **Protest and power in black Africa.**
Edited by Robert I. Rotberg, Ali A. Mazrui. New York: Oxford University Press, 1970. 1,274p. bibliog.

Pages 113 to 142 of this large work are devoted to a contribution by Sven Rubenson on the Ethiopian victory over the Italians at Adowa in 1896. Eritrea features heavily as the Italian base for invading Ethiopia. Good maps show the claims of both sides and the location of the battle.

111 **Imagining Ethiopia.**
John Sorenson. New Brunswick, New Jersey: Rutgers University Press, 1993. 216p. bibliog.

A research associate at both York (Canada) University's Centre for Refugee Studies and the University of Manitoba's Disaster Research Unit, Sorenson examines the issue of identity in the Horn of Africa. His approach is historical and focuses particularly on Eritrea and issues related to war, famine, media coverage and government. He includes a good bibliography.

112 **Caesar in Abyssinia.**
G. L. Steer. London: Hodder & Stoughton, 1936. 411p. maps.

This is the account of a British journalist who accompanied the Ethiopian armies during their heroic, but ultimately unsuccessful, defence against Italian aggression in

1935-36. The book was simultaneously published in Boston by Little, Brown & Co. in 1937 and contains maps.

113   **The Ethiopians.**
Edward Ullendorff.   London: Oxford University Press, 1973. 239p. bibliog.
This general history/geography of Ethiopia is particularly good on the peoples and pre-colonial history of Eritrea. Illustrations and a bibliography (page 203-19) are included.

Some records of Ethiopia.
See item no. 8.

Ethiopian itineraries circa 1400-1524.
See item no. 11.

Abysinnia and its people.
See item no. 13.

Narrative of the British mission to Theodore, king of Abyssinia.
See item no. 24.

Voyage sur la côte orientale de la Mer Rouge, dans le pays d'Adal et le royaume de Choa. (Journey to the east coast of the Red Sea, in the lands of Adal and the kingdom of Shewa).
See item no. 25.

A voyage to Abyssinia and travels into the interior of that country.
See item no. 27.

Voyages and travels to India, Ceylon, the Red Sea, Abyssinia and Egypt in the years 1802-1806.
See item no. 29.

Travels in Ethiopia.
See item no. 31.

Ethiopian journeys: travels in Ethiopia 1969-72.
See item no. 35.

Ethiopian adventure: from the Red Sea to the Blue Nile.
See item no. 41.

Evil days: thirty years of war and famine in Ethiopia.
See item no. 224.

Ethiopia at bay: a personal account of the Haile Sellassie years.
See item no. 248.

The foreign relations of Ethiopia 1642-1700: documents relating to the journeys of Khodja Murad.
See item no. 250.

The gentleman savage.
See item no. 293.

Histories of Eritrea

General

114 **L'Erythrée: une identité retrouvée.** (Eritrea: an identity recovered).
Nafi Hassan Kurdi. Paris: Karthala, 1994. 191p. maps. bibliog.
This French-language history of Eritrea under Italian and Ethiopian rule is particularly useful for its description of the development of liberation movements since 1952, superpower rivalry and the roles of the United Nations and the Organization of African Unity. Kurdi has included a preface by Michel Jobert, maps and a bibliography (pages 185-88).

115 **The history of Eritrea.**
Othman Salih Sabbe. Beirut: Dar Al-Masirah, [1970s]. 272p. bibliog.
Othman Salih Sabbe (alternatively spelled 'Uthman Salih Sabi or Othman Saleh Sabby) is perhaps the most prominent leader of the Eritrean struggle for independence. A founder of both the Eritrean Liberation Front (ELF) and the Eritrean People's Liberation Front (EPLF), Sabbe presents the history of his country from a nationalist's point of view. Translated from the Arabic by Mohammed Fawaz El Azem, this book contains a three-page bibliography.

Eritrea and Ethiopia: from conflict to co-operation.
See item no. 231.

The Horn of Africa: from war to peace.
See item no. 240.

Africa Report.
See item no. 300.

Africa Today.
See item no. 301.

The Economist.
See item no. 302.

Review of African Political Economy.
See item no. 333.

Colonial

116 **Operazioni militare nella colonie Eritrea.** (Military operations in the Eritrea colony).
Oreste Baratieri. In: *Miscellanea, Etiopia ed Eritrea.* Rome: Instituto per Africa, [1897-98].

The Italian operations that began on 15 December 1895 and continued through to the disastrous battle of Adowa are described in this piece. For a more expanded view of Italian activities in the 1890s, see Baratieri's *Memorie d'Africa 1892-1896*, which is an excellent 495-page account published in Genoa by Dioscuri in 1988. For an examination of earlier Italian actions see: E. Arimondi's article 'The Italian operations at Agordat' (*Journal of the Royal United Services Institution*, vol. 38 [1894]); *L'Eritrea com'e oggi* (Eritrea today) by Adolfo Rossi (Rome: Voghera Enrico, 1894. 199p.), an excellent eyewitness account of the battle of Agordat (21 December 1893), an engagement between the Italians and the Mahdists; and C. della Valle's unedited letter in Italian describing the battle of Agordat and its significance to the Italians, 'Tappe Italiano in Africa: la vittoria di Agordat (21 Dicembre 1893)' (Italian place in Africa: the victory of Agordat [21 December 1893]) (*Rivista Colonie Italiane*, vol. 7 [1933]).

117 **Eritrea 1941.**
A. J. Barker. London: Faber, 1966. 248p.

The British conquest of Eritrea early in the Second World War is described and analysed in detail in this book, which contains a foreword by General Sir William Platt. Illustrations, music, maps and photographs are provided.

118 **Da Assab a Dogali.** (From Assab to Dogali).
M. Camperio. Milan: Fratelli Dumolard, 1887. 128p.

A concise study of the establishment of the Italian colony of Eritrea, from the 1869 acquisition of the port of Assab to the 1887 battle of Dogali, is provided in this work, which is accompanied by a good folding map.

119 **Episodica guerriera di un battaglione Eritreo.** (War episodes of an Eritrean battalion).
Aldo Gatti. Rome: Barulli, 1969. 318p.

Eritrean participation on the Italian side in the Italo-Ethiopian War is discussed in this illustrated collection of memoirs. For earlier works see: Indro Montanelli's *XX Battaglione Eritreo* (The twentieth Eritrean battalion) (Milan, 1936), which provides a good description and history of an important Eritrean unit in the Italian invasion of Ethiopia between 1935 and 1936. Montanelli was an extremely prolific writer of Italian history, politics and foreign affairs. His general work *L'Italia nella Seconda Guerra Mondiale* (Italy in the Second World War) (Milan: RCS Rizzoli Libri, 1990) contains good background material on the Italo-Ethiopian War. Monte Meberro's *La promessa e l'offerta* (The promise and the offer) (Ravenna: Societa Tipo-Editrice Ravennate Mutilati, 1937) considers another Eritrean unit in this conflict: the Seventeenth Eritrean Battalion.

120 **L'impresa di Massawa – 1884-85.** (The Massawa company –
1884-85).
Carlo Giglio. Rome: Istituto Italiano per l'Africa, 1955. 188p.
Italy's foreign and colonial relations are dealt with in this history of Massawa at the
time the port became an Italian possession.

121 **L'Italia in Africa.** (Italy in Africa).
Edited by Carlo Giglio. Rome: Istituto Poligrafico dello Stato,
1958-66. 4 vols.
This authoritative work documents the history of Italian colonialism in Africa from
1857 to 1891. Hundreds of documents are presented, mainly in Italian, but also in
English and French. The first volume is particularly relevant to Eritrea, which is also
frequently mentioned in others.

122 **Les Italiens en Erythée.** (The Italians in Eritrea).
C. de la Jonquière. Paris: H. Charles-Lavauzelle, 1897. 352p.
French Marquis de la Jonquière examines the first forty years of Italian rule in Eritrea
in this well-written French-language text with illustrations and maps. Another French
view is provided in *La colonisation Italienne dans l'Erythrée* (Italian colonization in
Eritrea) by H. Dehérain (Paris: Hachette, 1904).

123 **A short history of Eritrea.**
Stephen H. Longrigg. London: Oxford University Press, 1945.
Reprinted, Greenwood Press, 1974. 188p. maps.
A British 'official' view of Eritrea is provided by Longrigg, who along with J. M.
Benoy was British administrator of Eritrea from 1941 to 1952. This work was
reprinted by Greenwood Press in 1974. Both printings include illustrations, maps and
a short list of sources.

124 **L'Eritrea dalle suo origini a l'anno 1901.** (Eritrea from its origins to
the year 1901).
B. Melli. Milan: U. Hoepli, 1902. 163p.
Melli provides a valuable examination of the first three decades of Italian colonization
in Eritrea. His earlier (1899) and longer (362p.) work, *La colonia Eritrea* (The Eritrea
colony) was published in Parma by L. Battei. For an earlier view, see *La
colonizzazione e l'ordinamento militare nell'Eritrea* (The colonization and military
rule of Eritrea) by G. B. Luciano (Rome: 1891). British and Ethiopian concerns with
Italian settlers are voiced in *Italian settlement policy in Eritrea and its repercussions
1889-1896* by Richard Pankhurst (*Boston University Papers on Africa*, vol. 1 [1964]).
A fascist view of Italian colonization in Eritrea is presented in C. Zaghi's *Le origini
della colonia Eritrea* (The origins of the Eritrea colony) (Bologna: L. Cappelli, 1934.
190p.).

125 **Assab e sui critici.** (Assab and its critics).
Giuseppe Sapeto. Genoa: P. Pellas, 1879.
Acting on behalf of the Rubattino Navigation Society, Italian Lazarist missionary
Giuseppe Sapeto purchased the port of Assab from local sultans at the end of the

1860s. This work lays out his arguments in favour of an Italian presence in the region and the need for refueling facilities to promote the commercial power of a newly unified Italy. See also 'Considerazioni sull'Italia e la baia di Assab' (Italian considerations and the bay of Assab) by F. Giustiani in *Miscellanea, Etiopia ed Eritrea* (Rome: Instituto per Africa, 1879).

126 **L'impero.** (The empire).
Tomaso Sillani. Rome: Rassegna Italiana Politica, 1937. 324p.

In spite of its bias towards Mussolini's fascism, this is a well-documented study of Eritrea and Somalia from an official Italian point of view. Containing numerous helpful maps and diagrams, the work is prefaced by Marshal Pietro Badoglio, commander of the Eritrea-based Italian forces which fought in northern Ethiopia in 1935-36. Sillani also edited *L'Africa Orientale Italiana: Eritrea e Somalia* (Italian East Africa: Eritrea and Somalia) (Rome: Rassegna Italiana Politica, 1933. 276p.), which has a preface by Emilio de Bono, Badoglio's predecessor.

127 **The centenary of Dogali: proceedings of the international symposium.**
Taddese Beyene, Taddesse Tamrat, Richard Pankhurst. Addis Ababa: Addis Ababa University Press, 1988. 344p.

This collection of papers was presented at the gathering of some twenty scholars, mainly from Addis Ababa University, to commemorate the Italian defeat at Dogali on 25 January 1887. They reflect on late 19th-century Ethiopian history, particularly the establishment of the Italian colony of Eritrea and Ras Alula's opposition to Italian colonialism.

128 **L'Eritrea-colonia 1890-1952: paesaggi, strutture, uomini del colonialismo.** (Eritrea – colony 1890-1952: landscape, structure, men of colonialism).
Irma Taddia. Milan: Franco Angeli, 1986. 429p. bibliog.

Written by an esteemed Italian scholar of Ethiopian and Eritrean history, this thorough, well-researched, but also concisely written, account of the establishment and development of Eritrea as an Italian colony is of prime importance to anyone interested in the colonial era. A good bibliography is included in this Italian-language book.

Assab e i Danachili: viaggio e studii. (Assab and the Danakil: journey and study).
See item no. 20.

Il diario Eritreo. (Eritrean diary).
See item no. 22.

Ost-Africanische Studien. (East Africa Studies).
See item no. 23.

L'Erythrée italienne. (Italian Eritrea).
See item no. 26.

Under the Red Sea sun.
See item no. 32.

Le drame éthiopien. (The Ethiopian drama).
See item no. 37.

Pearls, arms and hashish: pages from the life of a Red Sea navigator.
See item no. 38.

Notizie storiche e varie sulla missione evangelica Svedese dell'Eritrea: 1866-1916. (Historical and various knowledge on the Swedish evangelical mission in Eritrea).
See item no. 166.

La missione dei minori Cappuccini in Eritrea: 1894-1952. (The mission of the Capuchin minors in Eritrea: 1894-1952).
See item no. 167.

Viaggio e missione Cattolica fra i Mensa. (Travels and Catholic missions among the Mensa).
See item no. 169.

L'organizzazione sanitaria nell'Africa Italiana. (Health organization in Italian Africa).
See item no. 189.

Medical History.
See item no. 191.

Venti mesi di attivita chirurgica in Africa Orientale Italiana. (Twenty months of surgery in Italian East Africa).
See item no. 194.

Relazione sulla colonia Eritrea del regio commissario civale. (Report on the Eritrea colony by the royal civil inspector).
See item no. 202.

Italian colonialism: a case study of Eritrea.
See item no. 203.

Italian colonialism in Eritrea: 1882-1941.
See item no. 204.

Ethiopia and Eritrea: the last phase of the reunion struggle 1941-1952.
See item no. 205.

Eritrea: a colony in transition 1941-52.
See item no. 206.

L'ordinamento della giustizia e la procedure indigene in Etiopia e in Eritrea. (The regulation of justice and the indigenous procedures in Ethiopia and Eritrea).
See item no. 221.

L'ordinamento fondiario dell'Eritreo. (The basic regulation of Eritrea).
See item no. 222.

Italia e Etiopia. (Italy and Ethiopia).
See item no. 234.

Italy's foreign and colonial policy: 1914-1937.
See item no. 242.

Rassegna. (Review).
See item no. 290.

Ethiopia and Eritrea during the scramble for Africa: a political biography of Ras Alula (1875-1897).
See item no. 294.

The life and correspondence of Henry Salt.
See item no. 295.

Werner Münzinger Pascha: sein Leben und Wirken. (Werner Münzinger Pasha: his life and work).
See item no. 296.

Ventidue anni in Etiopia. (Twenty-two years in Ethiopia).
See item no. 297.

Chi è? dell'Eritrea. (Who's who in Eritrea?).
See item no. 298.

Africa Italiana. (Italian Africa).
See item no. 316.

Bollettino della Società Africana d'Italia. (Bulletin of the Italian African Society).
See item no. 319.

Bollettino della Società Geografica d'Italia. (Bulletin of the Italian Geographical Society).
See item no. 320.

Eritrea.
See item no. 322.

Proceedings of the Third International Conference on Ethiopian Studies.
See item no. 331.

Piccola bibliografia dell'Africa Orientale con speciale riguardo all'Eritrea e paesi confianti. (A short bibliography on East Africa with special regard to Eritrea and the surrounding countries).
See item no. 340.

Ethiopian rule

129 **Eritrea: revolution or capitulation.**
Anonymous. New York: Eritreans for Liberation in North
America/Association of Eritrean Women in North America, 1978.
114p.

This publication produced by Eritrean exiles is an ideologically leftist report on the
state of Eritrea's struggle against the Marxist government in Ethiopia. It also offers a
good introduction to the ideas of the various exile groups related to the EPLF. Other
publications by these groups are *Revolution in Eritrea: the Ethiopian military
dictatorship and imperialism* (1975) and *In defence of the Eritrean Revolution:
against Ethiopian social chauvinists* (1978). This organization also published a
narrative of the early armed opposition to Ethiopian rule: *Eritrea: the guerrillas of the
Red Sea* by J. L. Peninou in 1976.

130 **The Ethiopian revolution.**
Fred Halliday, Maxine Molyneux. London: Verso, 1980. 304p.

The Ethiopian Revolution of the mid-1970s and its effects on Eritrea are examined in
this book, which takes a leftist and generally pro-Ethiopian unionist stance. Maps and
a five-page bibliography are included. The book has been reprinted several times.

131 **Ethiopia: empire in revolution.**
Marina Ottaway, David Ottaway. New York: Africana, 1978. 250p.

This illustrated political history of the Ethiopian Revolution covers the early and mid-
1970s and includes information and an analysis of Eritrea's role in this profound
period of transformation.

**Ethiopian provincial and municipal government: imperial patterns and
post-revolutionary changes.**
See item no. 207.

**Land and peasants in imperial Ethiopia: the social background to a
revolution.**
See item no. 208.

Never kneel down: drought, development and liberation in Eritrea.
See item no. 209.

The dying lion: feudalism and modernization in Ethiopia.
See item no. 210.

Ethiopia: the modernization of autocracy.
See item no. 211.

Greater Ethiopia: the evolution of a multi-ethnic society.
See item no. 212.

Ethiopia: anatomy of a traditional polity.
See item no. 213.

The Ethiopian empire: federation and laws.
See item no. 220.

War for Independence

132 **The Ethiopian revolution: 1974-1987.**
Andargachew Tiruneh. Cambridge, Engand: Cambridge University
Press, 1993. 435p.
Subtitled 'a transformation from an aristocratic to a totalitarian autocracy', this
excellent study of the Ethiopian Revolution, including Eritrea's role in it, is part of
the London School of Economics Monograph Series in International Studies.

133 **Erythée: un peuple en marche.** (Eritrea: a people on the march).
Berhane Cahsai. Paris: Harmattan, 1985. 199p.
This work traces the history of Eritrea over the past century and a half. It is
particularly useful for its coverage of the national liberation movements which arose
following Eritrea's absorption into Ethiopia in the 1950s. The work contains sixteen
pages of plates.

134 **Against all odds.**
Dan Connell. Trenton, New Jersey: Red Sea Press, 1993. 309p.
maps.
Connell's chronicle of the Eritrean independence struggle extends from the Eritreans'
victories over the armies of Haile Selassie in the early 1970s to the rout of the Derg's
forces in 1991. His eyewitness account combines his observations as a journalist with
personal anecdotes, historical background and political analysis. Good illustrations
and maps are included.

135 **Behind the war in Eritrea.**
Basil Davidson, Lionel Cliffe, Bereket Habte Selassie. Nottingham,
England: Spokesman Books, 1980. 150p. bibliog.
This short work on the Eritrean People's Liberation Front and conditions in Eritrea
presents a good account of Eritrea's struggle against Ethiopian rule. It also contains a
useful bibliography.

136 **The long struggle of Eritrea for independence and constructive
peace.**
Edited by Basil Davidson, Lionel Cliffe, Bereket Habte Selassie.
Trenton, New Jersey: Red Sea Press, 1988. 215p.
The political movements and conditions of Eritrea before and during the country's
long war for independence are surveyed in this collection of short articles, which has
a strong pro-secessionist point of view. Illustrations and two maps are included.

137 **Eritrea: the national democratic revolution versus Ethiopian expansionism.**
Eritrean Liberation Front Foreign Information Center. Beirut: Eritrean Liberation Front, 1979. 107p.

This official publication of the Eritrean Liberation Front (ELF) traces the history of the movement's conflict with the Ethiopian government. A similar, earlier publication is *The Eritrean Revolution: 15 years of armed struggle*, dated 1 September 1977.

138 **The struggle for Eritrea, 1962-1978: war and revolution in the Horn of Africa.**
Haggai Erlikh. Stanford, California: Hoover Institution Press, 1983. 155p. map. bibliog.

A good short study of the early years of the Eritrean war for independence is provided in this book by a noted Israeli observer of Eritrean affairs. Erlikh discusses events from the 1962 dissolution of federal structures to the end of the 1970s, detailing both local events and their international ramifications. A short bibliography and map are included.

139 **Revolution in Eritrea: eyewitness reports.**
Edited by François Houtart. Rome: Research and Information Centre on Eritrea, 1980. 298p.

Illustrations and maps are included in this collection of testimonies of travellers in those areas of Eritrea under the control of the Eritrean People's Liberation Front (EPLF). A large proportion of the book is devoted to the history of the conflict and the EPLF. Two good articles on the early phases of the Eritrean struggle are 'Rumblings along the Red Sea' by J. F. Campbell in *Foreign Affairs* (April 1970); and 'The Eritrean Liberation Front: a close-up view' by Richard Lobban in the California Institute of Technology's *Munger Africana Library Notes*, no. 13 (1972).

140 **Eritrea: the struggle for independence.**
Robert Machida. Trenton, New Jersey: Red Sea Press, 1991. 169p.

This well-illustrated book constitutes a history of the Eritrean war for independence from 1962 to 1990. Photographs are included.

141 **The creation and termination of the Ethio-Eritrean Federation and the rise of Eritrea to national revolution.**
Yohannnes Okbazghi. Unpublished PhD thesis, University of Denver, Denver, Colorado, 1986. 472p.

Available on microfilm, Okbazghi's thesis is exceptional in its detailed treatment of the beginnings of the Eritrean struggle for independence in the 1960s.

142 **Eritrea: revolution at dusk, a pictorial rendering.**
Robert Papstein. Trenton, New Jersey: Red Sea Press, 1991. 169p. bibliog.

Papstein's book is one of the best collections of photographs on Eritrean subjects ever assembled. A short bibliography appears on p. 168.

143 **Eritrea: even the stones are burning.**
     Roy Pateman.   Trenton, New Jersey: Red Sea Press, 1990. 239p.
     bibliog.

Pateman has produced one of the best accounts of Eritrea's struggle for independence.
A short bibliography is included.

144 **The Eritrean war.**
     Roy Pateman.   *Armed Forces and Society*, vol. 17 (Fall 1990),
     p. 81-98.

In this article Pateman examines the effectiveness of the EPLF and the geopolitical
issues in the Horn of Africa and attempts to resolve the conflict peacefully. Also
offering insights into the early years of the Eritrean struggle for independence is
Richard Lobban's article 'The Eritrean War: issues and implications' *Revue
Canadienne des Etudes Africaines*, vol. 10, no. 2 (1976), p. 335-46.

145 **Eritrea: Africa's longest war.**
     David Pool.   London: Anti-Slavery Society, 1982. 79p.

David Pool, a British supporter of the Eritrean People's Liberation Front, has
chronicled the long history of Eritrean armed opposition to Ethiopian rule in this
revised edition of report number three of the Anti-Slavery Society's Human Rights
Series.

146 **The new insurgencies: anti-communist guerillas in the Third
     World.**
     Michael Radu.   New Brunswick, New Jersey: Transaction, 1990.
     306p.

This interesting book examines and compares the armed movements opposing leftist
governments in Eritrea, Angola, Mozambique, Cambodia, Afghanistan and Nicaragua
throughout the 1980s.

147 **Eritrea: the unfinished revolution.**
     Richard Sherman.   New York: Praeger, 1980. 197p. bibliog.

This study of the Eritrean struggle for independence from 1962 to the end of the
1970s is the author's revised PhD thesis (Brandeis University, 1979). Its seven-page
bibliography is particularly good on the opening phases of the guerrilla war.

Birth of a nation.
See item no. 1.

Eritrean journey.
See item no. 30.

African calliope.
See item no. 36.

The Eritrean Liberation Front's organizational structure outlined.
See item no. 214.

Class struggle and the problem of Eritrea.
See item no. 215.

Eritrea and Tigray.
See item no. 216.

The defeat of the derg and the establishment of new governments in Ethiopia and Eritrea.
See item no. 219.

Eritrea: a pawn in world politics.
See item no. 245.

Food and famine in Ethiopia: weapons against cultural diversity.
See item no. 269.

Surrender or starve: the wars behind the famine.
See item no. 273.

Eritrea Information.
See item no. 303.

Ethnic Groups and Folk Culture

148 **Household and society in Ethiopia.**
Dan Franz Bauer.   East Lansing, Michigan: Michigan State
University Press, 1985. 196p. bibliog.

An occasional paper of the Committee on Northeast African Studies of Michigan
State University's African Studies Center, Bauer's monograph presents an economic
and social analysis of Tigrayan social principles and household organization.
Virtually all of this material is applicable to highland Eritrea. A bibliography is found
on pages 181-87.

149 **The Abyssinians.**
David Buxton.   London: Thames & Hudson, 1970. 259p.

This is an excellent introduction to the peoples of the Horn of Africa by a Briton who
developed a keen interest in the area and an observant eye for local culture. Much of
the material concerns, or is relevant to, Eritrea. It includes several illustrations, maps
and a short bibliography.

150 **Africa Italiana: genti e costumi.** (Italian Africa: peoples and
customs).
Raffaele Corso.   Naples: R. Pironti, 1940. 188p. maps. bibliog.

The ethnology of Eritrea, Ethiopia, Somalia and Libya is surveyed in this book, which
is most valuable for its maps and extensive bibliography on pages 157 to 184. A good
earlier work in Italian is *Dall'Eritrea: lettere sui costumi Abissini* (From Eritrea:
letters on Abyssinian customs) by Francesco da Offeio, an Italian priest (Rome:
1904).

151   The Danakil: nomad's of Ethiopia's wasteland.
       V. Englebert.   *National Geographic Magazine*, vol. 137, no. 2
       (February 1970), p.186-211.
Excellent photographs and a text in the style of a travelogue make this piece a good
starting point for an examination of the Afar, the most studied of Eritrea's ethnic
groups. Another good, but difficult to acquire, article on the Afar is 'The tragedies of
three Afar girls' by Loren F. Bliese (*Ethiopianist Notes*, vol. 2, no. 3 [1978-79]).

152   **Impressions de voyage en Apharras.** (Impressions of a journey in
       the land of the Afars).
       F. Jousseaume.   Paris: J. B. Bailiere, 1914. 2 vols.
This illustrated French-language study of the Afar of Djibouti is equally applicable to
their kinsmen in Eritrea and Ethiopia.

153   **Peoples of the Horn of Africa: Somali, Afar and Saho.**
       I. M. Lewis.   London: International African Institute, 1955. 200p.
       map. bibliog.
This volume constitutes part one of the International African Institute's Ethnographic
Survey of Africa. It examines two Eritrean ethnic groups: the Afar and the Saho. A
folding map and a good bibliography (pages 177-94) are provided.

154   **Nomadic Peoples.**
       Montreal: 1980-present. irreg.
This journal devoted to the study of nomads is an expansion and continuation of the
newsletter of the Commission on Nomadic Peoples. Several articles on the Afar of
Eritrea and Ethiopia include: Ayele Gebre-Mariam's 'Labour inputs and time
allocation among the Afar' in no. 23 (1987) p. 37-56, and 'Livestock and economic
differentiation in Northeast Ethiopia: the Afar case' in no. 29 (1991) p. 10-20. 'The
camel and the household economy of the Afar' by Tegegne Teka in no. 29 (1991)
p. 31-41, is also of interest.

155   **A history of the Beja tribes of the Sudan.**
       Andrew Paul.   Cambridge, England: Cambridge University Press,
       1954. Reprinted, London: Frank Cass, 1971. 163p.
The Beja of the Sudan are not only related linguistically and culturally to numerous
Eritrean groups, but also frequently migrate into Eritrea itself. The 1971 reprint
contains a short bibliography.

156   **Le populazioni indigene dell'Eritrea.** (The indigenous population of
       Eritrea).
       Alberto Pollera.   Bologna: L. Cappelli, 1935. 337p.
Provides a good overview of the ethnic groups of Eritrea, in spite of its colonialistic
viewpoint. A useful bibliography is found on pages 327 to 330. Pollera wrote a number
of other works which have contributed to cultural and social knowledge of Eritrea,
including *La donna in Etiopia* (Women in Ethiopia) (Rome: Grafia SAI, 1922. 85p.),
which contained a number of photographs, and the well-illustrated *I Baria e i Cunama*
(The Baria and the Kunama) (Rome: Reale Societa Geografica, 1913. 285p.).

Travels in Ethiopia.
See item no. 31.

Risultati scientifici di un viaggio nella colonia Eritrea. (Scientific results of a journey in Eritrea colony).
See item no. 42.

L'Italia in Africa. (Italy in Africa).
See item no. 80.

The Ethiopians.
See item no. 113.

Greater Ethiopia: the evolution of a multi-ethnic society.
See item no. 212.

Journal of African Studies.
See item no. 327.

Journal of Ethiopian Studies.
See item no. 328.

Africa bibliography series: Northeast Africa.
See item no. 336.

Languages

157 Dictionary: Tigrinya-English.
Anonymous. Rome: Research and Information Centre on Eritrea, 1986. 637p.

The need for Eritrean language references grew out of the Eritrean independence struggle. Hence it is not surprising that this dictionary is the work of a branch of the EPLF. The Research and Information Centre on Eritrea also published a 718-page English-Tigrinya-Arabic dictionary in 1985.

158 Ethiopian language policy 1974-1981.
M. Lionel Bender. *Anthropological Linguistics*, vol. 27, no. 3 (June 1985), p. 273-79.

Bender provides a good, but brief, look at the continued attempts to 'Amharize' Eritrea and other parts of Ethiopia under the rule of the Derg.

159 Lingua Tigrina. (Tigrinya language).
Carlo Conti-Rossini. Milan: A. Mondadori, 1940. 278p.

This Tigrinya grammar was undertaken by the Ministry of Italian Africa as part of a series of works on the languages of the Horn of Africa. Conti-Rossini also wrote *Storia d'Etiopia* (A history of Ethiopia) (Milan: A. Lucini, 1928). Another good grammar of Tigrinya is Franz Praetorius' *Grammatik der Tigrinasprache in Abessinien* (Grammar of the Tigrinya language in Abyssinia) which was published in Halle in 1870, but is difficult to acquire.

160 Vocabulaire de la langue Tigre. (Vocabulary of the Tigre language).
Werner von Münzinger. Leipzig: T. O. Weigel, 1865. 93p.

Written by the Swiss trader/adventurer, who became the Egyptian governor of Massawa, this vocabulary was originally published as part of Dillman's *Lexicon Linguae Aethiopicae* the same year.

161 **Grammatica Tigrali-Italiana.** (Tigre-Italian grammar).
Francesco da Offeio. Rome: Casa Editrice Italiana, 1908. 190p.
This early Tigre grammar by an Italian missionary priest followed his 177-page grammatical work of one year earlier *Grammatica della lingua Tigrai* (Grammar of the Tigre Language) (1907).

162 **A Tigrinya chrestomathy.**
Edward Ullendorff. Stuttgart: F. Steiner, 1985. 242p.
This collection of Tigrinya phrases, letters and other texts is accompanied by a Tigrinya-English glossary, grammatical tables and a short select bibliography. Ullendorff's work is an essential text for those wishing to study the languages of highland Eritrea. For a recent specialized work on Tigrinya phonology, see 'Labialization and the so-called sibilant anomaly in Tigrinya' by Rainer M. Voigt (*The Bulletin of the School of Oriental and African Studies*, vol. 51, no. 3 [1988], p. 525-36).

Journal of Ethiopian Studies.
See item no. 328.

Africa bibliography series: Northeast Africa.
See item no. 337.

Religion

Christianity

163 **Christentum am Rotem Meer.** (Christianity on the Red Sea).
Franz Altheim, Ruth Stiehl. Berlin: De Gruyter, 1971 & 1973.
2 vols.
This well-researched and extensive church history written in German includes Eritrea.

164 **The Church of Ethiopia: a panorama of history and spiritual life.**
Ethiopian Orthodox Church. Addis Ababa: Ethiopian Orthodox
Church, 1970. 97p.
This introduction to the Coptic Orthodox tradition of Eritrea and Ethiopia is good,
concise and official. A similar work is *The Church of Ethiopia: an introduction to the
contemporary church* (Addis Ababa: Ethiopian Orthodox Church, 1973). Three other
useful general works on Abyssinian Christianity are Ephraim Isaac's *The Ethiopian
Church* (Boston: H. N. Sawyer, 1968); E. C. Molnar's *The Ethiopian Orthodox
Church: a contribution to the ecumenical study of less known Eastern churches*
(Pasadena, California: Bloy House Theological School, 1969); and *The Ethiopian
Orthodox Church* edited by Aymro Wondmagegnehu and Joachim Motovu (Addis
Ababa: The Ethiopian Orthodox Mission, 1970). Of an even more general nature but
good for the information it provides on the background and status of the Eritrean and
Ethiopian churches is *The Orthodox Church* by Timothy Ware (London: Penguin,
1963). For a sociological look at the Orthodox church in both Eritrea and Ethiopia,
see Fred Goricke and Friedrich Heyer, *The Orthodox Church of Ethiopia as a social
institution* (Frankfurt: Westdeutscher Verlag, 1976. 241p.). Numerous more specific
works have also been published, including *The cult of saints in the Ethiopian Church*
by Tito Lipisa (Rome: Typis Pontificiae Universitatis Gregorianae, 1963) and *The
liturgy of the Ethiopian Church* by Marcos Daoud (Addis Ababa: 1954) which takes a
detailed look at church rites. An even deeper view is found in 'The sacraments of
baptism and chrism in the rite of the Coptic Orthodox Church' by Bishop Gregorious

in *Abba Salama*, vol. 2 (1971). Information on Ethiopian monastic literature is contained in 'Pergamene di Debra Dammo' (The Debra Dama parchments) by Carlo Conti-Rossini (*Rivista Studi Orientali*, vol. 19 [1940]).

165 **The church history of Ethiopia.**
Michael Geddes.   London: R. Chiswell, 1696. 488p.
The title of this early work is misleading on a number of accounts. In the first place, Geddes focuses quite narrowly on the Dominicans and other Roman Catholic orders and their missions. Secondly, most of the material is related to Eritrea and Tigray, rather than to the more inner reaches of Ethiopia.

166 **Notizie storiche e varie sulla missione evangelica Svedese dell'Eritrea: 1866-1916.** (Historical and various knowledge on the Swedish evangelical mission in Eritrea).
Jonds Iwanson.   Asmara: Missione Evangelica Svedese, 1918.
One of a few works on the Swedish Lutheran missionaries who were active in Eritrea at the end of the 19th century.

167 **La missione dei minori Cappuccini in Eritrea: 1894-1952.** (The mission of the Capuchin minors in Eritrea: 1894-1952).
Metodio da Nembro.   Rome: Institutum Historicum (Capuchin Order), 1953. 503p.
Constitutes an excellent Italian-language history of Capuchin missionary activity in Eritrea in the late 19th and early 20th century. A somewhat more personal narrative is found in Father da Nembro's *Vita missionaria in Eritrea* (Missionary life in Eritrea) (Rome, 1953). Two useful early accounts of the Capuchins in Eritrea are *I Cappuccini nella colonia Eritrea: ricordi* (The Capuchins in the Eritrea colony: records) by Father Francesco da Offeio (Rome, 1910); and *Il Cappuccino Eritreo: episodii drammatici della querra d'Africa* (The Eritrean Capuchins: a dramatic episode in the conversion of Africa) by Ernesto Mezzabotta (Rome, 1896).

168 **Lo stato etiopico e la sua chiesa.** (The Ethiopian state and its church).
Alberto Pollera.   Rome: Societa Editrice d'Arte Illustrata, 1926. 373p.
The Ethiopian Empire, the Coptic Orthodox Church and the relationship between the two are examined in this well-illustrated book by one of the most important Italian scholars in the field of North-east African studies.

169 **Viaggio e missione Cattolica fra i Mensa.** (Travels and Catholic missions among the Mensa).
Giuseppe Sapeto.   Rome: Propaganda Fide, 1857. 528p.
This Italian-language account of Roman Catholic missionaries in Eritrea also includes a description of the country and its history, geography, religion and natural history. Appendices contain documents in Italian, Greek and Ethiopic languages.

170   **The Christian church and missions in Ethiopia.**
J. S. Trimingham.   London: World Dominion Press, 1950. 73p. maps.
A fine general work on Christianity in Eritrea, Djibouti and Somalia, containing
folding maps.

171   **The Church of Ethiopia: the national church in the making.**
Yolande Mara.   Asmara: Il Poligrafico, 1972. 180p. maps. bibliog.
This book was published in English and a number of other languages as part of an
effort to reaffirm the position of the Coptic Orthodox church in Ethiopian, and
particularly Eritrean, life. Maps and a short bibliography are included.

A voyage to Abyssinia.
See item no. 14.

Travels of the Jesuits in Ethiopia.
See item no. 17.

Assab e i Danachili: viaggio e studii. (Assab and the Danakil: journey and
study).
See item no. 20.

**The question of the union of churches in Luso-Ethiopian relations: 1500-
1632.**
See item no. 98.

The lost empire: the story of the Jesuits in Ethiopia, 1555-1634.
See item no. 99.

Assab e sui critici. (Assab and its critics).
See item no. 125.

Traditional Ethiopian church education.
See item no. 280.

Music in the Coptic church of Egypt and Ethiopia.
See item no. 285.

Churches in rock: early Christian art in Ethiopia.
See item no. 287.

Religious art of Ethiopia.
See item no. 289.

**Proceedings of the Third International Conference on Ethiopian
Studies.**
See item no. 331.

Islam

172 **Islam in tropical Africa.**
I. M. Lewis. London: Oxford University Press, 1966. Reprinted,
London: Hutchinson, 1980. 310p. maps.
Substantial material on Eritrea is contained within the 92-page Introduction of this
authoritative book. Maps are included.

173 **La necropoli islamica di Dahlak Kebir nei Mar Rossi.** (The Islamic
necropolis on Grand Dahlak in the Red Sea).
G. Oman. *Africa*, vol. 29 (1974).
One of the first areas of the Horn of Africa to come under Muslim influence was the
Dahlak archipelago. This article examines the remains of early Islamic colonies on
those rugged and sun-scorched islands east of Massawa.

174 **In the shadow of conquest.**
Said S. Samatar. Trenton, New Jersey: Red Sea Press, 1992. 163p.
bibliog.
This is a Muslim's study of Islam in colonial north-eastern Africa. A short
bibliography is provided.

175 **Islam in Ethiopia.**
J. S. Trimingham. London: Frank Cass, 1976. 299p. maps.
Trimingham's book is probably the best English-language text available on Islam in
the Horn of Africa. The original edition was published by Oxford University Press in
1952. Maps, illustrations and genealogical tables accompany this work. A good
example of an early article on Islam by a European missionary is 'Islam in Eritrea and
Abyssinia' by Jonas Iwanson (*Moslem World*, vol. 18 [January 1928]).

**Ethiopia and the Red Sea: the rise and decline of the Solomonic dynasty
and Muslim-European rivalry in the region.**
See item no. 89.

The Ethiopian slave trade and its relation to the Islamic world.
See item no. 90.

Social Conditions

176 **African company town: the social history of a wartime planning experiment.**
Ephraim Gordon Ericksen. Dubuque, Iowa: W. C. Brown, 1964. 144p. maps.
Examines the social conditions of Gura, a small town in the Akele Guzai province. Illustrations and maps are included.

177 **Life in liberated Eritrea.**
Joseph Marando. Rome: Research and Information Centre on Eritrea, 1987. 128p. maps.
Using maps and photographs and sub-titled 'portrait of a people who are constructing a new society', this book offers a vivid picture of life in Eritrea during a critical time in the country's struggle for independence. The material was gathered in those areas of the country which were under the control of the liberation movements and the social, political and economic conditions are discussed and illustrated. The text is produced in English, French and Spanish.

L'Italia in Africa. (Italy in Africa).
See item no. 80.

Household and society in Ethiopia.
See item no. 148.

Journal of Refugee Studies.
See item no. 179.

Refugees and development in Africa: the case of Eritrea.
See item no. 180.

Disposable people? The plight of refugees.
See item no. 181.

World Refugee Survey.
See item no. 183.

Female genital mutilation: proposals for change.
See item no. 184.

Women and revolution in Eritrea.
See item no. 185.

The challenge road: women and the Eritrean Revolution.
See item no. 188.

The Ethiopia Observer.
See item no. 305.

Refugee Issues

178 **Out of the war zone.**
Anne Fry. *Social Work Today*, vol. 22, no. 16 (13 December 1990), p. 29-31.
Concentrating on a refugee unit in the borough of Hillingdon, Fry looks at social work among young Eritrean refugees in London.

179 **Journal of Refugee Studies.**
Oxford: 1988-present. quarterly.
As the journal of the Refugee Studies Programme of Oxford University, this quarterly publication has included much information on Eritrea. Among the more noteworthy articles are 'Social differentiation among Eritrean refugees in Eastern Sudan: the case of Wad El Hileau' by Johnathan B. Bascom (vol. 2, no. 4 [1989]) and 'I have a name' by L. A. McSpadden and Helene Moussa (vol. 6, no. 3 [1993]), which studies the gender dynamics in asylum and in the resettlement of Eritrean refugees in North America.

180 **Refugees and development in Africa: the case of Eritrea.**
Gaim Kibreab. Trenton, New Jersey: Red Sea Press, 1987. 304p. bibliog.
During the 1970s and 1980s, more than half a million Eritreans fled into the Sudan as a result of the fighting, famine and instability in their own land. This well-researched study of the economic and social conditions of Eritrean and Ethiopian refugees in the Sudan is a revision of the author's doctoral thesis. A bibliography appears on pages 293 to 304.

181 **Disposable people? The plight of refugees.**
Judy A. Mayotte. Maryknoll, New York: Orbis Books, 1992. 347p. bibliog.
Mayotte compares case-studies of refugees in Eritrea, Afghanistan and Cambodia in this excellent book. A useful and extensive bibliography appears on pages 305-35.

182   **Refugees.**
Geneva: January 1982-present. monthly.

This publication of the Office of the United Nations High Commissioner for Refugees has included numerous articles related to the Eritrean refugee issue. A good recent example is 'Eritrea: life at the end of the road' (September 1992).

183   **World Refugee Survey.**
New York: United States Committee for Refugees, 1980-present. annual.

Frequently noting the conditions of Eritrean refugees, this annual survey published an excellent article on Eritrean refugees in the aftermath of the struggle for independence: 'Beyond famine: new dynamics in post-war Ethiopia and Eritrea' by Jeffrey Clark (1992).

Country report: Eritrea.
See item no. 2.

New Internationalist.
See item no. 311.

Women's Issues

184 **Female genital mutilation: proposals for change.**
Efua Dorkenoo, Scilla Elworthy.   London: Minority Rights Group,
1992. 43p.

Originally published in December 1980 under the title *Female circumcision, excision
and infibulation*, this monograph is the best short work available on female genital
mutilation. It includes material on Eritrea and much from other countries which also
applies to Eritrean women. Another useful publication on this topic is *The Hosken
report: genital/sexual mutilation of females* by Fran P. Hosken (Lexington,
Massachusetts: WIN News, 1982. revised and enlarged third edition). One of the
earliest works on female genital mutilation to be written in a European language is an
interesting French-language article which is specific to Eritrea: 'Sur l'infibulation ou
mutilation des organs génitaux de la femme chez les peuples de la Mer Rouge et du
Golfe d'Aden' (On the infibulation and mutilation of female genital organs among the
peoples of the Red Sea and Gulf of Aden) by F. Jousseaume (*Revue d'Anthropologie*,
vol. 4 [1889]).

185 **Women and revolution in Eritrea.**
National Union of Eritrean Women.   Rome: National Union of
Eritrean Women, 1980. 30p.

The social conditions and political status of Eritrean women are discussed in this
short monograph. The NUEW was a wing of the EPLF, which allowed far greater
recognition of women in its ranks than any other mass political organization in North-
east Africa.

186 **A painful season/a stubborn hope.**
Abeba Tesfagiorgis.   Trenton, New Jersey: Red Sea Press, 1992. 210p.

Sub-titled 'the odyssey of an Eritrean mother', this book constitutes a woman's
personal look at the Ethiopian occupation of Eritrea, the struggle for independence,
political prisoners and the diaspora of Eritrean refugees.

187 **Zar and buda in northern Ethiopia.**
Joseph Tubiana.   In: *Women's medicine: the Zar-Bori cult in Africa and beyond.*   Edited by I. M. Lewis, Ahmed Al-Safi, Sayyid Hurreiz. Edinburgh: Edinburgh University Press, 1991, p. 19-33.

The Zar are totally female cults found in Eritrea and throughout North-east Africa. Folk medicine, spirit possession and spiritual healing among women in these groups are the subjects of this study for the International African Institute.

188 **The challenge road: women and the Eritrean Revolution.**
Amrit Wilson.   London: Earthscan; Trenton, New Jersey: Red Sea Press, 1991. 207p. maps. bibliog.

The views, roles and conditions of women in Eritrea are examined in this interesting book. Illustrations, maps and a helpful bibliography (pages 198-204) are included. A good article on the role of women in Eritrea's struggle for independence is 'Organising women within a national liberation struggle: the case of Eritrea' by Worku Zerai in *Economic and Political Weekly* (vol. 29, no. 44 [29 October 1994], p. 63). Another post-independence view of the status of women can be found in Lori Grinker's 'The main force' in *Ms. Magazine* (May/June 1992), p. 46-51. For information on the status of women historically, see: 'The traditional role and status of women in imperial Ethiopia' by Anna Ferryhough (*Journal of the Steward Anthropological Society*, vol. 13, no. 2 [1982], p. 69-81).

Country report: Eritrea.
See item no. 2.

Le populazioni indigene dell'Eritrea. (The indigenous population of Eritrea).
See item no. 156.

Journal of Refugee Studies.
See item no. 179.

Emergent Eritrea.
See item no. 256.

The Economist.
See item no. 302.

Health

189 **L'organizzazione sanitaria nell'Africa Italiana.** (Health
organization in Italian Africa).
Giuseppe Bucco, Angelo Natoli.   Rome: Istituto Poligrafico dello
Stato, 1965. 371p. bibliog.

This excellent survey of public health in Eritrea and Somalia by Bucco and Libya by
Natoli includes illustrations and a good bibliography. Additional information can be
found in Henry R. O'Brien's article, 'Mapping a program of public health for
Ethiopia and Eritrea' (*Public Health Reports*, vol. 68, no. 10 [October 1953]).

190 **Malaria in Africa.**
Michael J. Colbourne.   London: Oxford University Press, 1966. 115p.
maps. bibliog.

Malaria is endemic in much of Eritrea and in this work Colbourne provides a good
overview of the disease in Eritrea and Africa in general. Maps, diagrams and a
bibliography are included. Numerous other publications on Malaria with relevance to
Eritrea have been published. *Malariology* by Mark F. Boyd (Philadelphia: Saunders,
1949. 1,643p.) is the classic work of sixty-five contributors, which is described as 'a
comprehensive survey of all aspects of this group of diseases from a global
standpoint'. *The resistance of falciparum malaria in Africa to 4-aminoquinlines and
antifolates* by Allan Schapira (Copenhagen: Kaleidoscope, 1990. 63p.) is a study of
the growing resistance of malaria parasites to anti-malarial drugs, a concern in
Eritrea. Finally *Migrants and malaria* by R. M. Prothero (London: Longmans, 1965.
142p.) is a study of malaria among African migrant labourers, which includes maps,
illustrations and a bibliography.

191 **Medical History.**
London: 1957- present. quarterly.

Based on both Eritrean and Ethiopian data, Richard Pankhurst wrote a number of
articles for this journal describing the historical incidence of a number of diseases,

including smallpox (vol. 9, no. 4 [1965]); typhus (vol. 12, no. 3 [1968]); cholera (vol. 12, no. 4 [1968]); rabies (vol. 14, no. 4 [1970]); and influenza (vol. 21, no. 3 [1977]).

192 **Traditional attitudes towards mental illness in Ethiopia.**
S. Petros, E. Schier. *Curare*, vol. 12, nos. 3-4 (1989), p. 161-67.
This interesting, unique and well-researched article is equally applicable to Eritrea.

193 **Mending lives.**
Tom Rayner. *Nursing Times*, vol. 89, no. 51 (22 December 1993), p. 30.
The injuries and disabilities stemming from Eritrea's long struggle for independence are examined in this article. Particular attention is paid to handicapped EPLF fighters.

194 **Venti mesi di attivita chirurgica in Africa Orientale Italiana.**
(Twenty months of surgery in Italian East Africa).
Giuseppe Rotolo. Milan: Bocca, 1939. 236p.
Rotolo's memoirs contribute to an understanding of the medical history of both Eritrea and Ethiopia and show the Italo-Ethiopian War and subsequent occupation from a different perspective than the usual accounts. The Italian colonial authorities in Eritrea appear to have excelled best in the field of health and along with the establishment of hospitals, clinics and doctors, a good deal of research was conducted by Italians. *Missione scientifica in Eritrea per lo studio della radiazione penetrante* (Scientific mission to Eritrea for the study of penetrating radiation) by B. Rossi, I. Ranzi and S. de Benedetti (Rome: Ministero dell'Educazione Nazionale, 1934. 605p.) was a study of the medical and other effects of prolonged exposure to sunlight and provides a good example of the sort of medical and scientific work conducted by the Italians in Eritrea.

195 **Political violence and Eritrean health care.**
Lois Sabo, Joachim Kibirige. *Social Science and Medicine*, vol. 28, no. 7 (1989), p. 677.
The medical effects of three decades of war are examined in this excellent article. Slightly more recent and equally good is 'Eritrean medicine' by Thomas Keneally (*Medical Journal of Australia*, vol. 153, no. 5 [September 1990], p. 241-60).

Preliminary data on the Anopheles gambiae complex (diptera: Culicidae) in some sites in western Eritrea.
See item no. 56.

Zar and buda in northern Ethiopia.
See item no. 187.

Politics

General

196 **Conflict and peace in the Horn of Africa: federalism and its alternatives.**
Edited by Murray Forsyth, Peter Woodward. Aldershot, England: Dartmouth Publishing, 1994. 130p. bibliog.

This is a collection of papers presented at a conference sponsored by the University of Leicester's Centre for Federal Studies and the Council for Civil Liberties in Ethiopia, held in Leicester in December 1990. The topics covered included the prospects for peace, political stability and economic progress in Eritrea, Ethiopia, Somalia and the Sudan and the benefits of creating federal structures of government and federal links between countries in the region. Good bibliographical lists are appended.

197 **Peasants and nationalism in Eritrea.**
Jordan Gebre-Medhin. Trenton, New Jersey: Red Sea Press, 1989. 220p. bibliog.

Eritrean politics, with particular reference to rural areas, is the subject of this recent work, which also contains a critique of traditional Ethiopian studies. A lengthy bibliography is found on pages 199-214. A similar, but more general, work on peasant politics is Gebru Tareke's *Ethiopia: power and protest: peasant revolts in the twentieth century* (Cambridge, England: Cambridge University Press, 1991. 272p.).

198 **Ethnic nationalism and political conflict: a comparative study of the Basque country and Eritrea.**
Siamak Khatami. *Scandinavian Journal of Development Alternatives*, vol. 9, no. 4 (December 1990), p. 49-65.

This unusual, thought-provoking article compares the conflict between Eritreans and the Ethiopian central government with the difficult relationship between the Basques and the central government of Spain.

199   **Nationalism and self-determination in the Horn of Africa.**
Edited by I. M. Lewis.   London: Ithaca Press, 1983. 226p.

The ethnic groups and national liberation movement of Eritrea are discussed in numerous contexts in Lewis's collection. Chapters relevant to Eritrea include 'Self-determination and the OAU' by James Mayall (p. 77-92); 'The changing idiom of self-determination in the Horn of Africa' by Sally Healy (p. 92-109); 'Competing views of national identity in Ethiopia' by Alessandro Triulzi (p. 111-27); 'Eritrean nationalism' by David Pool (p. 175-93); and 'Centralism and the Ethiopian PMAC' by Patrick Gilkes (p. 195-211). A short bibliography is included.

200   **Class and revolution in Ethiopia.**
John Markakis, Nega Ayele.   Nottingham, England: Spokesman Books, 1978. Reprinted, Trenton, New Jersey: Red Sea Press, 1986. 191p.

A leftist examination and explanation of the causes of the Ethiopian revolution is developed in this book.

201   **No medicine for the bite of the white snake: notes on nationalism and resistance in Eritrea: 1890-1940.**
Tekeste Negash.   Uppsala, Sweden: University of Uppsala Press, 1986. 99p. bibliog.

The beginnings of Eritrea's separatist attitudes are explored in this short monograph, which includes a bibliography on pages 95-99.

Birth of a nation.
See item no. 1.

Country report: Eritrea.
See item no. 2.

An African winter.
See item no. 46.

The invention of Ethiopia.
See item no. 104.

Protest and power in black Africa.
See item no. 110.

Imagining Ethiopia.
See item no. 111.

The history of Eritrea.
See item no. 115.

Ethiopia, Eritrea, Somalia, Djibouti: country reports, analyses of economic and political trends.
See item no. 255.

Africa Confidential.
See item no. 299.

Africa Report.
See item no. 300.

The Ethiopia Observer.
See item no. 305.

New African.
See item no. 309.

New Statesman and Society.
See item no. 310.

New Internationalist.
See item no. 311.

The World Today.
See item no. 312.

Africa Affairs.
See item no. 314.

Horn of Africa.
See item no. 325.

Journal of Modern African Studies.
See item no. 329.

Proceedings of the Fifth International Conference on Ethiopian Studies.
See item no. 332.

Review of African Political Economy.
See itcm no. 333.

Colonial administration

202 **Relazione sulla colonia Eritrea del regio commissario civale.**
(Report on the Eritrea colony by the royal civil inspector).
Ferdinando Martini.   Rome: Tipografia della Camera dei Deputati,
1913-14. 4 vols.

Martini has reproduced the records of the Italian colony of Eritrea presented to the Italian Chamber of Deputies by the first Italian governor of Eritrea, after he had left office. Another work describing early Italian administration is Giacinto Rossi's *La prefettura Eritrea* (The Eritrea prefecture) published in Genoa in 1895.

203 **Italian colonialism: a case study of Eritrea.**
Yemane Mesghenna.   Lund, Sweden: University of Lund, 1988.
256p. bibliog.

The author's PhD thesis on Italian colonial rule from 1890 to 1941 was reproduced as number 58 of the University of Lund's Skrifter utgivna av Ekonomisk-historiska foreningen. An extensive bibliography is found on pages 237 to 253.

204 **Italian colonialism in Eritrea: 1882-1941.**
Tekeste Negash.   Uppsala, Sweden: Uppsala University Press, 1987.
217p. bibliog.

This political history of Eritrea is number 148 in Uppsala University's historical studies series. It provides an interesting account of the Italian presence in the country and includes a good bibliography on pages 195-211.

205 **Ethiopia and Eritrea: the last phase of the reunion struggle 1941-1952.**
Sylvia Pankhurst, Richard Pankhurst.   Woodford Green, England: Lalibela House, 1953. 360p.

A detailed, pro-Ethiopian unionist view of the end of European colonialism in Eritrea is found in this work, which includes a number of photographs. Issues related to the British administration, Eritrean unionists and Italian settlers are discussed. Similiar themes are examined in Sylvia Pankhurst's 1952 *New Times and Ethiopia News* article 'Eritrea on the eve: the past and future of Italy's "first born" colony, Ethiopia's ancient sea province' (also reprinted as a book) and in her earlier book, *British policy in Eritrea and Northern Ethiopia* (Woodford Green, England: Lalibela House, 1946).

206 **Eritrea: a colony in transition 1941-52.**
Gerald K. N. Trevaskis.   London: Oxford University Press, 1960.
Reprinted, London: Greenwood Press, 1975. 137p. maps.

This political history of Eritrea during the era of British administration was issued under the auspices of the Royal Institute of International Affairs. A good earlier work is David Mathew's *Ethiopia: a study of a polity* (London: Eyre & Spottiswoode, 1947. 254p.), which provides an illustrated political history of Ethiopia from 1540 to 1935, written during the era of British administration in Eritrea when efforts were first underway to unite the former Italian colony with the Ethiopian Empire.

Africa Orientale Italiana. (Italian East Africa).
See item no. 21.

Il diario Eritreo. (Eritrean diary).
See item no. 22.

Colonial postscript: diary of a district officer.
See item no. 39.

Italy in Africa.
See item no. 76.

La missione dell'Italia in Africa. (Italy's mission in Africa).
See item no. 77.

The Italo-Abyssinian war, the operations: Massawa-Addis Ababa.
See item no. 78.

L'impérialisme colonial italien de 1870 à nos jours. (Italian colonial imperialism from 1870 to the present day).
See item no. 79.

L'Italia in Africa. (Italy in Africa).
See item no. 80.

Africa Orientale Italiana: cinquanta anni dopo. (Italian East Africa: fifty years later).
See item no. 82.

L'Africa Italiana. (Italian Africa).
See item no. 84.

Storia e politica coloniale Italiana: 1869-1937. (Italian colonial history and politics: 1869-1937).
See item no. 86.

La guerra d'Etiopia. (The war in Ethiopia).
See item no. 95.

The coming of the Italian-Ethiopian war.
See item no. 96.

The civilizing mission: a history of the Italo-Ethiopian war of 1935-1936.
See item no. 97.

Black shirt, black skin.
See item no. 100.

The Ethiopian War 1935-1941.
See item no. 101.

L'Italia in Africa. (Italy in Africa).
See item no. 121.

Les Italiens en Erythée. (The Italians in Eritrea).
See item no. 122.

A short history of Eritrea.
See item no. 123.

L'impero. (The empire).
See item no. 126.

The centenary of Dogali: proceedings of the international symposium.
See item no. 127.

L'Eritrea-colonia 1890-1952: paesaggi, strutture, uomini del colonialismo. (Eritrea – colony 1890-1952: landscape, structure, men of colonialism).
See item no. 128.

Ethiopian administration

207 Ethiopian provincial and municipal government: imperial patterns and post-revolutionary changes.
John M. Cohen, Peter H. Koehn. East Lansing, Michigan: Michigan State University Press, 1980. 317p.

This overview of Imperial Ethiopia's sub-national governmental system is valuable for its reference to Eritrea during the years 1952 to 1974. It was produced by the African Studies Center of Michigan State University as monograph number 9 of their Ethiopian Series.

208 Land and peasants in imperial Ethiopia: the social background to a revolution.
John M. Cohen, Dov Weintraub. Assen, Netherlands: Van Gorcum, 1975. 115p. maps. bibliog.

Land tenure, agriculture and government economic policies prior to the Ethiopian Revolution of the mid-1970s are the major topics of this work, which seeks to explain the causes of the revolution. Much of the material in this book is relevant to Eritrea, either directly or indirectly. Maps and a short bibliography are included.

209 Never kneel down: drought, development and liberation in Eritrea.
James Firebrace, Stuart Holland. Nottingham, England: Spokesman for War on Want, 1984. 192p. maps. bibliog.

Firebrace and Holland were two of the most prominent British supporters of the Eritrean People's Liberation Front. Their work includes sections on the historical and political context of the Eritrean struggle, economic and social development and an interview with the vice general secretary of the EPLF. The preface was written by Neil Kinnock. Useful appendices with documents relating to Eritrean history are included, along with four good maps, photographs and a bibliography.

210 The dying lion: feudalism and modernization in Ethiopia.
Patrick Gilkes. London: Friedmann; New York: St. Martin's Press, 1975. 307p. bibliog.

The political and economic conditions of Eritrea under Ethiopian control are examined by British journalist Gilkes. Issues related to land tenure, political traditions and militant opposition are analysed in particular detail. A bibliography appears on pages 293 to 298.

211 **Ethiopia: the modernization of autocracy.**
Robert L. Hess.   Ithaca, New York: Cornell University Press, 1970.
292p. maps. bibliog.
Part of Cornell's Africa in the Modern World series, this book provides an excellent, but dated, look at Ethiopia at the time when it included Eritrea. Ranging from trade unions to commerce and the media, numerous aspects of Ethiopian life are described and analysed. The significance of the 1960 coup, the role of education and the Eritrean liberation movements are particularly emphasized. A good bibliography and five maps accompany this work.

212 **Greater Ethiopia: the evolution of a multi-ethnic society.**
Donald N. Levine.   Chicago: University of Chicago Press, 1974.
229p. maps. bibliog.
Levine looks at the ethnic politics in the Horn of Africa, particularly among the Amhara, the Oromo and the peoples of Eritrea, at a time of great instability and change. Included are charts, maps and a bibliography (pages 211-22).

213 **Ethiopia: anatomy of a traditional polity.**
John Markakis.   London: Oxford University Press, 1974. 409p. maps.
bibliog.
Maps and a ten-page bibliography accompany this excellent work on the political and social condition in Ethiopia, including Eritrea, before the Ethiopian Revolution. To fit the Ethiopian situation in a broader context, see *African kingships in perspective: political change and modernization in monarchical settings*, edited by René Lemarchand (London: Frank Cass, 1977. 325p.). Dividing African monarchies into four groups: theocratic kingdoms – Ethiopia; stratified kingdoms – Rwanda and Burundi; ethnic kingdoms – Swaziland and Lesotho; and incorporated kingdoms – Buganda, Ankole and Ijebu-Yoruba, this work analyses the impact of change on these systems and the subsequent decline of African monarchical regimes.

Eritrean journey.
See item no. 30.

Ethiopian journeys: travels in Ethiopia 1969-72.
See item no. 35.

Ethiopian language policy 1974-1981.
See item no. 158.

Peasants and nationalism in Eritrea.
See item no. 197.

Nationalism and self-determination in the Horn of Africa.
See item no. 199.

Class and revolution in Ethiopia.
See item no. 200.

No medicine for the bite of the white snake: notes on nationalism and resistance in Eritrea: 1890-1940.
See item no. 201.

Conflict with Ethiopia

214 **The Eritrean Liberation Front's organizational structure outlined.**
Anonymous. *US Joint Publications Research Service Translations
on Africa* (Washington DC), document no. 71246 – 1941. (1978).
The background on the ELF is given in this translation of an article that appeared in
Al-Thawrah Al-Iritriyah (Beirut: ELF, 6 June 1978.)

215 **Class struggle and the problem of Eritrea.**
Ethiopian Revolution Information Center. Addis Ababa: Ethiopian
Revolution Information Center, 1979. 139p. map.
This Marxist justification for Ethiopian political and military action against Eritrea is
similar in tone to the Ethiopian Revolution Information Center's twenty-four-page
work, *The Ethiopian Revolution and the problem of Eritrea* (July 1977). The equally
Marxist viewpoint of the Derg is presented in *The red star multi-faceted
revolutionary campaign* by Ethiopian dictator Mengistu Haile Mariam (Addis Ababa:
Berhanema Selam Press, 1982).

216 **Eritrea and Tigray.**
Colin Legum, James Firebrace. London: Minority Rights Group,
1983. 19p. bibliog.
This excellent monograph on the conflict between the Eritrean people and the
Ethiopian government is the most recent revision in a series of reports on the region
(1971, 1973 and 1976). Unlike previous editions which focused solely on Eritrea, this
publication considers Tigray as well. Topics include an overview of the country and
its people and sections on: the Ethiopian case; the Eritrean case; the origins of the
Eritrean political movement; the period of federation with Ethiopia; liberation fronts;
Eritrea under Mengistu; international dimensions; and prospects for a solution.

Red tears: war, famine and revolution in Ethiopia.
See item no. 102.

Eritrea: revolution or capitulation.
See item no. 129.

The Ethiopian revolution.
See item no. 130.

Ethiopia: empire in revolution.
See item no. 131.

The Ethiopian revolution: 1974-1987.
See item no. 132.

Erythée: un peuple en marche. (Eritrea: a people on the march).
See item no. 133.

Against all odds.
See item no. 134.

Independence

217 Reflections on the future political system of Eritrea.
Bereket Habte Selassie.   Washington DC: Eritreans for Peace and
Democracy, 1990. 70p.

This 'working paper' examines the possibilities for a stable political system in an
independent Eritrea. Bereket Habte Selassie is a particularly authoritative figure: a
British-trained Eritrean lawyer who was Ethiopia's Attorney General (1962-67);
mayor of Harar, Ethiopia (1968-70); vice minister of the interior in Ethiopia (1970-
72); an official with the World Bank (1972-74); an exile; an activist on behalf of
Eritrean refugees; and currently a professor at Howard University in Washington DC.

218 The fate of Africa: trial by fire.
Jeremy Harding.   New York: Simon & Schuster, 1993. 368p.

This is a revised edition of British journalist Harding's earlier work, *Small wars,
small mercies*, which features six African nations in which the author sees 'the
unfinished business of national liberation'. A vivid portrait of Eritrea is presented in
chapter six.

**219 The defeat of the derg and the establishment of new governments
in Ethiopia and Eritrea.**
Paul B. Henze.   Santa Monica, California: Rand Corporation, 1992.
33p.

Henze's short report examines the dramatic events of 1991-93 which established a
new order in the Horn of Africa. It includes bibliographical references. Also by the
same author and publishers are earlier monographs including *Eritrean options and
Ethiopia's future* (1989).

Eritrea and Ethiopia: from conflict to co-operation.
See item no. 231.

The Horn of Africa: from war to peace.
See item no. 240.

Constitutions and legal system

220 The Ethiopian empire: federation and laws.
Nathan Marein.   Rotterdam, Netherlands: Royal Netherlands Printing
and Lithographing, 1955. 456p.

Written by an Israeli lawyer who advised the Ethiopian Imperial Government, this
interesting and comprehensive overview of the Ethiopian legal system pays particular
attention to Eritrea, which at the time of publication had recently been 'federated'
with Ethiopia. The Eritrean judicial system is described in part two. This work

superseded Marein's earlier tome *The judicial system and the laws of Ethiopia* (Rotterdam: Royal Netherlands Printing and Lithographing, 1951. 277p.). Both of these books were intended to be practical guides for judges and lawyers.

221 **L'ordinamento della giustizia e la procedure indigene in Etiopia e in Eritrea.** (The regulation of justice and the indigenous procedures in Ethiopia and Eritrea).
Alberto Pollera. Rome: Tipografia Nazionale di G. Bertero, 1913. 86p.

Presents the results of an official Italian survey of the native legal system of Eritrea and Ethiopia at this time.

222 **L'ordinamento fondiario dell'Eritrea.** (The basic regulation of Eritrea).
Renzo Sertoli Salis. Padua: CEDAM, 1932. 189p.

Sertoli Salis offers a good reference to Italian colonial law as it applied to land tenure, property and agriculture in Eritrea in the early 1930s. He also wrote a number of other works related to legal affairs, including: *Nozioni di diritto coloniale* (Knowledge of colonial rights) (Milan: Edizioni G U F, 1938) and *La figura giuridica del Vice Governatore Generale dell'Africa Orientale Italiana* (Judicial features of the Vice Governor General of Italian East Africa) (Padua: CEDAM, 1939).

Paideuma.
See item no. 330.

Human Rights

223 **Amnesty International Reports.**
Amnesty International. London: Amnesty International, 1975-present.
annual.
Amnesty International provides in its annual reports a review of human rights
violations worldwide. Eritrea has been covered in articles on Ethiopia. Appendices
relating to the international protection of human rights are useful references. This
publication replaced the earlier *Amnesty International Annual Reports* (1961-74).

224 **Evil days: thirty years of war and famine in Ethiopia.**
Human Rights Watch Africa Committee. Boston: Human Rights
Watch, 1991. 386p.
Monitoring Ethiopia's human rights record from 1961 to 1991, this report separates
recent Eritrean and Tigrayan history into four periods: scorched earth (1961-77); total
war (1978-84); starving Tigray (1984-88); and the politics of relief (1989-91). Maps
are provided. Also good on this topic is *Surrender or starve* by Robert D. Kaplan
(Boulder, Colorado: Westview, 1988. 188p.).

225 **The Eritrean case.**
International League for the Rights and Liberation of Peoples.
Rome: International League for the Rights and Liberation of Peoples,
1982. 405p. bibliog.
Records the proceedings of a conference held in Milan on 24-26 May 1980 by the
Permanent People's Tribunal of the International League for the Rights and
Liberation of Peoples. The document is accompanied by illustrations and a
bibliography.

226 **The southern Sudan and Eritrea: aspects of wider African problems.**
Godfrey Morrison.   In: *The fourth world: victims of group oppression*.   Edited by Ben Whitaker.   New York: Schocken, 1973. 342p.
This chapter on minority issues in the Horn of Africa is one of eight which details the field-work of the London-based Minority Rights Group.

227 **Genocide convention, intentional starvation and Ethiopian famine in the Eritrean war for independence.**
Jean E. Zeiler.   *The Georgia Journal of International and Comparative Politics*, vol. 19, no. 3 (September 1989), p. 589-612.
This article examines the applicability of the United Nations' Genocide Convention to the Ethiopian government-imposed famine in Eritrea in the 1980s.

Surrender or starve: the wars behind the famine.
See item no. 273.

Index on censorship.
See item no. 307.

Foreign Relations

228   **The Red Sea: prospects for stability.**
Abdel Majid Farid.   London: Croom Helm, 1984. 173p. bibliog.
An Arab view of regional politics in the Horn of Africa is presented in this work, which was sponsored by the Arab Research Centre. A short bibliography is included. Also discussing the Arab involvement in Eritrea, as well as wide international issues, is Frank Boyce's 'The internationalizing of internal war: Ethiopia, the Arabs and the case of Eritrea' (*Journal of International and Comparative Studies*, vol. 5, no. 3 [1972]).

229   **Red Sea politics.**
Mordechai Abir.   London: International Institute for Strategic
Studies, 1972. 52p. (Conflicts in Africa).
Abir's work on conflict in the Horn of Africa is monograph number ninety-three of the Adelphi Papers, a series jointly organized by the University of Paris, the University of London's School of Oriental and African Studies and the International Institute for Strategic Studies. Also worth reading is Abir's article 'The contentious Horn of Africa' (*Conflict Studies*, vol. 24 [1972]).

230   **The Red Sea region: local actors and the superpowers.**
Roberto Aliboni.   Syracuse, New York: Syracuse University Press,
1985. 143p. bibliog.
Aliboni examines the geopolitics of the Horn of Africa in this useful book which contains a foreword by Boutrous Boutrous Ghali. A bibliography appears on pages 121-29.

231   **Eritrea and Ethiopia: from conflict to co-operation.**
Edited by Amare Tekle.   Trenton, New Jersey: Red Sea Press, 1994.
229p.

This book was the result of a discussion among Eritrean scholars at the November 1989 African Studies Association conference in Atlanta, Georgia. Noting the likelihood of Eritrean independence, this group explored the possible relationships which could develop between Eritrea and Ethiopia. Discussions and recommendations centred on: the elimination of the causes of conflict; the inauguration of a durable peace based on justice, freedom and equality; and the creation of a co-operative relationship between Eritrea and Ethiopia as a necessary first step for the creation of a 'Horn of Africa Community'.

232   **Conflict and intervention in the Horn of Africa.**
Bereket Habte Selassie.   London: Monthly Review Press, 1980. 211p.

Provides a good analysis of conflicts in the Horn of Africa during the 1960s and 1970s.

233   **Eritrea and the United Nations and other essays.**
Bereket Habte Selassie.   Trenton, New Jersey: Red Sea Press, 1988.
350p. bibliog.

This important work lays out the legal argument for Eritrean nationhood and examines Eritrea's international status up to the point where the Eritreans have occupied all but the cities of their homeland.

234   **Italia e Etiopia.** (Italy and Ethiopia).
Giuliano Cora.   Florence: Università degli Studi di Firenze, Centro
Studi Coloniali, 1951. 31p.

This monograph is publication number thirty-nine of the University of Florence's Centre for Colonial Studies. It is essentially a diplomatic history of Italy and the Horn of Africa.

235   **Beyond conflict in the Horn.**
M. Doornbos, L. Cliffe, A. G. M. Ahmed, J. Markakis.   Trenton,
New Jersey: Red Sea Press, 1992. 242p.

Resulting from the International Workshop on the Prospects for Peace, Recovery and Development in the Horn of Africa at the Institute of Social Studies in the Hague (19-23 February 1991), this collection looks at the prospects for peace, recovery and development in Ethiopia, Somalia, Eritrea and the Sudan.

236   **Without troops and tanks: humanitarian intervention in Ethiopia
and Eritrea.**
Mark Duffield, John Prendergast.   Lawrenceville, New Jersey: Red
Sea Press, 1994. 214p. bibliog.

In this recent book the authors present an excellent description of international relief efforts and the issues surrounding them. A short bibliography is included.

237 **War clouds in the Horn of Africa.**
Tom J. Farer. New York: Carnegie Endowment for International
Peace, 1976. 157p.

This overview of the problems of Eritrea, Ethiopia and Somalia during the period
leading up to the Ethiopian Revolution is accompanied by maps and a four-page
bibliography.

238 **Ethiopia and Eritrea: a documentary study.**
Habtu Ghebre-Ab. Trenton, New Jersey: Red Sea Press, 1993. 264p.

The full texts of forty major documents relating to Eritrea's relations with Ethiopia,
Italy, the United Nations and other foreign powers and entities are presented in this
excellent reference work. They range from the 1888 treaty between Italy and the
Sultan of Aussa to the 1955 revisions of Ethiopia's constitution. This is not only an
invaluable reference tool on the historical aspects of Eritrea's foreign relations, but
also a good source of background material on both Eritrean and Ethiopian politics and
their effects on diplomacy.

239 **The Horn of Africa.**
Edited by Charles Gurdon. New York: St. Martin's Press, 1994.
122p.

The first three chapters of this collection have particular relevance for Eritrea: chapter
one by Patrick Gilkes discusses the effects of secession on Ethiopia and Somalia;
chapter two by Paul Henze looks at the importance of economics to the region's
future; and chapter three by Alex DeWaal examines the changed role of Ethiopia in
the region.

240 **The Horn of Africa: from war to peace.**
Paul B. Henze. London: Macmillan, 1991. 248p.

Henze examines Ethiopia and Eritrea in the pre-Derg era. The work is accompanied
by photographs and maps.

241 **The Horn of Africa in continuing crisis.**
Colin Legum, Bill Lee. New York: Africana, 1979. 166p.

Maps and bibliographical references accompany this analysis of the conflicts between
Ethiopia on the one hand and Somalia and Eritrea on the other. The work also
includes an important chapter, 'Cuba: the new Communist power in Africa' by
Zdenek Cervenka & Colin Legum. The international aspects of these conflicts are
explored in some detail. The same authors also wrote the similar work *Conflict in the
Horn of Africa* (London: Rex Collings, 1977).

242 **Italy's foreign and colonial policy: 1914-1937.**
Maxwell H. H. Macartney, Paul Cremona. London: Oxford
University Press, 1938. 353p.

Composed following the Italian invasion of Ethiopia, this analysis of Italian foreign
policy in Africa, Europe and the Mediterranean features Eritrea frequently.

243 **The legality of secessions: the case of Eritrea.**
Minasse Haile. *Emory International Law Review*, vol. 8, no. 2
(Fall 1994), p. 479-99.
The international legal provisions related to the separation of Eritrea from Ethiopia
are explained in this well-researched, important piece.

244 **On the shores of the Bab al-Mandab: Soviet diplomacy and
regional dynamics.**
Nimrod Novik. Philadelphia, Pennsylvania: Foreign Policy Research
Institute, 1979. 83p.
This monograph examines Soviet policy in the Horn of Africa in the light of
Moscow's maritime concerns. Bibliographical sources are included.

245 **Eritrea: a pawn in world politics.**
Okbazghi Yohannes. Gainesville, Florida: University of Florida
Press, 1991. 331p.
Eritrea's role in superpower politics between 1941 and 1991 is the subject of this
recent work. Earlier publications on superpower roles in Eritrea include *Super powers
in the Horn of Africa* by Madan M. Sauldie (New York: APT Books, 1987. 252p.) and
*The Soviet Union in the Horn of Africa: the diplomacy of intervention and
disengagement* by Robert G. Patman (Cambridge: Cambridge University Press, 1990.
411p.).

246 **Soviet and American influence in the Horn of Africa.**
Marina Ottaway. New York: Praeger, 1982. 187p.
The role of the superpowers in the Horn of Africa is the subject of this book which
has a three-page bibliography. More important to a current understanding of Eritrea is
Ottaway's 'Mediation in a transitional conflict: Eritrea' in the *Annals of the American
Academy of Political and Social Science* (vol. 518 [November 1991], p. 69-81).

247 **Security Dialogue.**
Oslo: 1992-present. quarterly.
Published in London by Sage for the International Peace Research Institute in Oslo,
this journal has seen the publication of a number of articles on Eritrean/Ethiopian
relations. The most important are 'Closing the mediation gap: the Ethiopia/Eritrea
experience' by Dayle Spencer, William Spencer and Honggang Yang (vol. 23, no. 3
[September 1992], p. 89) and 'The challenge of mediation in internal wars: reflections
on the INN experience in the Ethiopian/Eritrean conflict' by Hizkias Assefa (vol. 23,
no. 3 [September 1992], p. 101).

248 **Ethiopia at bay: a personal account of the Haile Sellassie years.**
John H. Spencer. Algonac, Michigan: Reference Publications, 1984.
397p.
An employee of the Ethiopian foreign ministry for many years, Spencer traces
Ethiopian foreign policy from the 1935 Italian invasion to the deposition of Emperor
Haile Selassie in 1974. Much attention is paid to the post-Second World War disposal
of Eritrea and other former Italian colonies.

249 **Ethiopia-French territory of the Afars and Issas boundary.**
United States Department of State. Washington DC: United States
Department of State, 20 February 1976.

The Eritrea-Djibouti border is described and delineated in this document which is
International Boundary Study number 154 of the United States State Department's
Bureau of Intelligence and Research.

250 **The foreign relations of Ethiopia 1642-1700: documents relating to
the journeys of Khodja Murad.**
Emeri Johannes van Donzel. Leiden, Netherlands: Nederlands
Historisch-Archaeologisch Instituut te Istanbul, 1979. 304p. maps.

Khodja Murad was an Armenian trader in the service of the Ethiopian Emperor. This
absorbing account of his diplomatic and trading missions, most of which were routed
through Eritrea, was written by a Dutch orientalist. The significance of this work lies
in its depiction of the late 17th-century Horn of Africa as a centre of much activity, a
view which challenges the conventional belief that Abyssinia was isolated from the
rest of the world. Maps and twelve plates are included.

251 **United Nations 1993 consolidated inter-agency appeal: Eritrea.**
Anonymous. New York: Special Emergency Programme for the
Horn of Africa (SEPHA), January 1993. 54p.

Noting the impoverished and disaster-prone condition of Eritrea, this United Nations
report is the first step in a co-ordinated international effort to rebuild the country now
that peace has arrived.

Country report: Eritrea.
See item no. 2.

Italy in Africa.
See item no. 76.

Storia e politica coloniale Italiana: 1869-1937. (Italian colonial history and
politics: 1869-1937).
See item no. 86.

La guerra d'Etiopia. (The war in Ethiopia).
See item no. 95.

The coming of the Italian-Ethiopian war.
See item no. 96.

The civilizing mission: a history of the Italo-Ethiopian war of 1935-1936.
See item no. 97.

Black shirt, black skin.
See item no. 100.

The Ethiopian War 1935-1941.
See item no. 101.

Italy's conflict with Ethiopia: the facts of the case.
See item no. 109.

Caesar in Abyssinia.
See item no. 112.

Eritrea 1941.
See item no. 117.

L'impresa di Massawa – 1884-85. (The Massawa company – 1884-85).
See item no. 120.

The Eritrean war.
See item no. 144.

The new insurgencies: anti-communist guerillas in the Third World.
See item no. 146.

Conflict and peace in the Horn of Africa: federalism and its alternatives.
See item no. 196.

Nationalism and self-determination in the Horn of Africa.
See item no. 199.

Amnesty International Reports.
See item no. 223.

The Eritrean case.
See item no. 225.

The southern Sudan and Eritrea: aspects of wider African problems.
See item no. 226.

Genocide convention, intentional starvation and Ethiopian famine in the Eritrean war for independence.
See item no. 227.

Africa Today.
See item no. 301.

The Ethiopia Observer.
See item no. 305.

The World Today.
See item no. 312.

Horn of Africa.
See item no. 325.

Journal of Ethiopian Studies.
See item no. 328.

Journal of Modern African Studies.
See item no. 329.

Review of African Political Economy.
See item no. 333.

Ethiopia and the Italo-Ethiopian conflict.
See item no. 335.

The Economy and Economic Development

252 African Business.
London: IC Publications, 1966-present. monthly.
This British-based magazine, formerly named *African Development*, regularly reports on Eritrean political, economic and business news. Some examples are 'Eritrea: solar power brings short-term energy relief' (May 1994, p. 18) and 'Eritrea: the financial hub of the Horn' (October 1994, p. 37).

253 Agriculture, industry and commerce in Ethiopia and Eritrea.
Edited by K. A. Cherian.   Asmara: [n.p.], 1957. 106p.
The economic potential and conditions of Eritrea following the establishment of the Ethiopian-Eritrean federation are surveyed in this short book, which was issued by an unlisted publisher in Asmara.

254 Development and Change.
The Hague: 1969-present. quarterly.
Featuring Eritrea in a number of issues, this journal of the Hague's Institute of Social Studies was published by Mouton until 1975 when publication was taken over by Sage in London. A good article on Eritrea is 'The impact of war and the response to it in different agrarian systems in Eritrea' by Lionel Cliffe (vol. 20, no. 3 [July 1989], p. 373-90).

255 Ethiopia, Eritrea, Somalia, Djibouti: country reports, analyses of economic and political trends.
The Economist.   London: Economist Intelligence Unit, quarterly.
This specialized publication of *The Economist* offers up-to-date economic, financial and political information for business and economic research. Accompanied by careful analysis and numerous statistics, this quarterly publication records and predicts possible trends in Eritrea and the other countries of the Horn of Africa.

256 **Emergent Eritrea.**
Edited by Gebre Hiwet Tesfagiorgis. Trenton, New Jersey: Red Sea Press, 1993. 304p.

A series of conference papers presented on 22-24 July 1991 in Asmara, this book explores the challenges of economic development in newly-independent Eritrea. Sponsored by the Provisional Government of Eritrea and the refugee organization Eritreans for Peace and Democracy in North America, chapters include analyses of regional co-operation, government plans, education, labour policy, women's issues, agriculture, the environment, finance, banking, trade, industry, water resources, harbours, petroleum, construction, technological capabilities, information technology and the mass media. Opening remarks by Haile Woletensae and a keynote address by the Eritrean president Afewerki are included. Lists of important references follow each chapter.

257 **The primacy of economics for the future of the Horn of Africa.**
Paul B. Henze. Santa Monica, California: Rand Corporation, 1992. 23p.

The economic and political conditions and outlook for Eritrea and Ethiopia after their division are discussed in this short monograph.

258 **An economic history of Ethiopia: 1800-1935.**
Richard K. Pankhurst. Addis Ababa: Haile Selassie I University Press, 1968. 772p. maps. bibliog.

This is by far the best historical work on the economy of the Horn of Africa prior to the 1935 Italian invasion of Ethiopia. As the most important trading routes all passed through Massawa and Assab, Eritrea features very heavily in this work, which contains illustrations and an excellent bibliography on pages 726 to 746.

259 **Rassegna Economica della Colonie.** (The Colonial Economic Review).
Rome: 1913-40. annual.

A number of important articles appeared in this publication in the 1930s, including 'I prodotti dei suolo coltivati e spontanei in Eritrea' (The production of cultivated and native soil in Eritrea) by I. Baldrati (vol. 20 [1932]) and 'Boschi e servizio forestale in Eritrea' (Wood and forestry service in Eritrea) by R. Guiolotti (vol. 22 [1934]). Two unattributed articles of importance are 'L'industria della pesca in Eritrea nel 1932' (The fishing industry in Eritrea in 1932) (vol. 21 [1933]) and 'L'andamento d'agricultura in Eritrea durante il 1933' (Agricultural trends in Eritrea during 1933) (vol. 22 [1934]).

260 **Roman economic policy in the Erythra Thalassa.**
Steven E. Sidebotham. Leiden: E. J. Brill, 1986. 226p. maps. bibliog.

A revision of the author's 1981 PhD thesis at the University of Michigan, this excellent book describes Roman trade and politics in the Red Sea region, including Eritrea, from 30 BC to 217 AD. Maps, illustrations and fifteen pages of plates accompany this work, as well as an extensive and useful bibliography on pages 189-215.

261   **Politica economica fascista in Africa Orientale Italiana.** (Fascist
      political economy in Italian East Africa).
      Renato Trevisani.   Rome: Edizioni di Politica Sociale, 1937. 117p.

In this publication, Trevisani outlines proposals for the creation of a fascist corporate
economy in Eritrea.

A plague of locusts.
See item no. 66.

L'Italia in Africa. (Italy in Africa).
See item no. 80.

Household and society in Ethiopia.
See item no. 148.

**African company town: the social history of a wartime planning
experiment.**
See item no. 176.

Life in liberated Eritrea.
See item no. 177.

Refugees and development in Africa: the case of Eritrea.
See item no. 180.

The Economist.
See item no. 302.

Esploratore Commerciale. (Commercial Exploration).
See item no. 304.

New African.
See item no. 309.

Finance and Trade

262 **La colonia Eritrea e i suoi commerci.** (The Eritrea colony and its trade).
Ennio Q. M. Alamanni. Turin: F. Bocca, 1891. 911p.
Eritrea's 19th-century trade is thoroughly examined in this large, detailed work with tables and folding maps.

263 **La vita commerciale Etiopica e la circolazione monetaria Eritrea.**
(Ethiopian commercial life and Eritrean monetary circulation).
Alberto Pollera. Rome: Istituto Coloniale Italiano, 1926. 78p.
Pollera offers a good, concise study of Eritrea's trade and monetary policies under the Italians, prior to the Mussolini era.

Agriculture, industry and commerce in Ethiopia and Eritrea.
See item no. 253.

Emergent Eritrea.
See item no. 256.

Industry and Mining

264 **L'industria in Africa Orientale Italiana.** (Industry in Italian East
Africa).
Confederazione Generale dell'Industria Italiana. Rome: USILA,
1939. 401p. maps.

Although excessively optimistic and clearly affected by the politics of Mussolini's
Italy, this description of industry in Eritrea, Ethiopia and Somalia has remained an
important work on the region's economy. Of interest to economic historians are the
maps, diagrams and huge appendix of relevant sections of the Italian codes governing
industry in African colonies.

265 **The mineral resources of Africa.**
Nicolas de Kun. Amsterdam; New York: Elsevier, 1965. 740p.
bibliog.

This reference work on the mineral resources of Africa and their exploitation is
accompanied by illustrations, maps and a good bibliography (p. 683-95). Though not
as detailed, some updated information is found in de Kun's *The mineral economics of
Africa* (Amsterdam; New York: Elsevier, 1987. 345p.). For more recent and more
specific information, particularly on the prospects of gold and petroleum production,
see: 'Mineral resources of Eritrea' by Camillo Premoli in *The Mining Magazine*
(vol. 170, no. 3 [March 1994]).

266 **Risorse minerarie dell'Africa Orientale: Eritrea, Etiopia, Somalia.**
(Mineral resources of East Africa: Eritrea, Ethiopia, Somalia).
Luigi Usoni. Rome: Ispettorato Generale Minerario – Ministero
dell'Africa Italiana, 1952. 553p. maps. bibliog.

This official Italian government study (in Italian) is one of the best sources of
information on the mines and mineral resources of Eritrea. It is accompanied by a
short bibliography and very good illustrations and maps.

Hot brines and recent heavy metal deposits in the Red Sea: a geochemical and geophysical account.
See item no. 51.

Agriculture, industry and commerce in Ethiopia and Eritrea.
See item no. 253.

Emergent Eritrea.
See item no. 256.

Agriculture

267 **Land tenure in Eritrea.**
Ambaye Zekarias. Addis Ababa: Addis Printing Press, 1966. 80p.
The system of land tenure and the issue of land reform have long been major features of both agriculture and politics in Eritrea and Ethiopia. Issues and laws related to land tenure are examined in this well-researched monograph. A bibliography is included on pages 79 and 80. *State and land in Ethiopian history* by Richard Pankhurst (Addis Ababa: Haile Selassie I University Press; London: Oxford University Press, 1966. 211p.) constitutes a detailed, well-documented history of land tenure in Ethiopia and Eritrea from ancient times to the early 20th century. For a shorter study, see 'Land tenure on the Eritrean Plateau' by S. F. Nadel (*Africa*, vol. 18, no. 1 [January 1946]). A more recent article on Eritrean land tenure is Irma Taddia's 'The land tenure system in the Eritrean Highlands according to European colonial sources' which appears on pages 299-308 of *The Proceedings of the Eighth International Conference of Ethiopian Studies* (Addis Ababa: Institute of Ethiopian Studies, 1989).

268 **New perspectives on the origins of food production in Ethiopia.**
Steve A. Brandt. In: *From hunters to farmers.* Edited by J. D. Clark, S. A. Brandt. Berkeley, California: University of California Press, p. 173-90.
Brandt's chapter in this unique work considers the transition to settled agriculture in the highlands of Eritrea and Ethiopia.

269 **Food and famine in Ethiopia: weapons against cultural diversity.**
Jason W. Clay. *Cultural Survival Quarterly*, vol. 9, no. 4 (September 1985), p. 47-50.
Jason Clay of the Harvard-based organization Cultural Survival International pursued extensive research in various parts of the Horn of Africa during the famine crisis of the early 1980s. *Cultural Survival Quarterly* also featured Clay's 'Refugees flee Ethiopian collectivization' (vol. 10, no. 2 [March 1986], p. 80-85). He also wrote

'Anthropologists and human rights: activists by default' (*Human Rights and Anthropology* [1988], p. 115-20).

270 **Il servizio veterinario nell'Africa Italiana.** (The veterinary service in Italian Africa).
Edited by Gaetano Conti. Rome: Istituto Poligrafico dello Stato, 1965. 239p. bibliog.

The provision of veterinary medicine in colonial Eritrea is examined in this well-researched book. It contains illustrations, maps and a good bibliography.

271 **The Eritrean durrah odyssey.**
Frits Eisenloeffel, Inge Ronnback. Utrecht, Netherlands: SOH Publications, 1983. 87p.

This is a report on emergency famine relief aid in the EPLF-occupied zones of Eritrea. *Durrah* is the local word for *sorghum*, the staple food of many North-east African diets.

272 **Concession agriculture in Eritrea.**
Haile Wolde Emmanuel. *Ethiopian Geographical Journal*, vol. 2, no. 1 (January 1964).

A good study of large-scale agriculture is provided in this short article. Two other pieces useful in expanding on related topics are: L. Massa's article 'Le piante da frutto coltivate in Eritrea' (The planting of cultivated fruits in Eritrea) *Agricoltura Coloniale*, vol. 28 (1934) and 'Some aspects of Eritrean fruit production' by David R. H. Jones in *Sudan Notes and Records*, vol. 46 (1965). A good bibliography on agricultural topics related to Eritrea is *Contribution to an Italian bibliography on Ethiopia 1935-50* (Florence: Istituto Agronomico per l'Africa Italiana, 1952).

273 **Surrender or starve: the wars behind the famine.**
Robert D. Kaplan. Boulder, Colorado: Westview Press, 1988. 188p.

Kaplan's work is one of the best available on the background to famine in the Horn of Africa. Another short work on this subject is the eighty-five-page monograph *Ethiopia, the politics of famine* (New York: Freedom House, 1990). See also Richard S. Scobie's *War and famine in the Horn of Africa* (Boston: Unitarian Universalist Service Committee, 1985. 20p.), which is a report of an investigation into the famine, food relief and food supply issues which faced Eritrea and the Sudan in the early and mid-1980s. These findings are the result of a tour from 15 January to 5 February 1985.

274 **The politics of famine in Ethiopia and Eritrea.**
Paul Kelemen. Manchester, England: University of Manchester, Department of Sociology, 1985. 35p.

As Manchester Sociology Occasional Paper number thirteen, this brief report seeks out the underlying political reasons behind famine in the Horn of Africa in the early 1980s.

275 **The cultivated sorghums of Ethiopia.**

H. F. Rouk, H. Mengesha. Alemaya, Ethiopia: Research Department of College of Agriculture, [1960s].

Rouk and Mengesha were in charge of the Central Experiment Station of the Imperial Ethiopian College of Agricultural and Mechanical Arts, near Dire Dawa, Ethiopia. A number of their monographs are relevant to the agriculture and natural history of Eritrea. This monograph which discusses the staple food, sorghum, is Experimental Station Bulletin number six.

276 **An introduction to t'ef (Eragrostis abyssinica schard).**

H. F. Rouk, H. Mengesha. Alemaya, Ethiopia: Research Department of College of Agriculture, [1960s].

Teff, or T'ef, is a type of millet cultivated and consumed in only the highland areas of Eritrea and Ethiopia. It is the basic starch food of the Abyssinian diet. This is Experimental Station Bulletin number twenty-six of the Central Experiment Station of the Imperial Ethiopian College of Agricultural and Mechanical Arts.

277 **Agriculture in the tropics.**

C. C. Webster, P. N. Wilson. London: Longman, 1980. 640p. bibliog. (Tropical Agriculture Series.)

This is one of the best general texts available in English on tropical agriculture. An analysis of crops and techniques is accompanied by illustrations and a forty-page bibliography. Much material is applicable to Eritrea.

A plague of locusts.
See item no. 66.

Nomadic Peoples.
See item no. 154.

Peasants and nationalism in Eritrea.
See item no. 197.

Never kneel down: drought, development and liberation in Eritrea.
See item no. 209.

Agriculture, industry and commerce in Ethiopia and Eritrea.
See item no. 253.

Development and Change.
See item no. 254.

Emergent Eritrea.
See item no. 256.

Journal of Ethiopian Studies.
See item no. 328.

Education

278 **Free at last to build a new nation.**
Dave Hampson. *Times Educational Supplement*, no. 4,025
(20 August 1993), p. 9.
This short article examines the newly established Eritrean educational system, a
system which includes strict national standards and religious instruction. Noting the
high rate of illiteracy and other problems facing the Ministry of Education, Hampson
describes the improvements which were made in schools and adult literacy
programmes between 1991 and mid-1993. An earlier, similar article in this well-
respected publication was Jill Rutter's 'A fitful start after years of brutal neglect' (2
April 1993, p. 19), which discusses the problems stemming from a lack of
international recognition prior to the 1993 referendum and shortages of teachers,
supplies and money.

279 **Eritrea: freedom of expression and ethnic discrimination in the
educational system.**
Human Rights Watch Africa Committee. Boston: Human Rights
Watch, 1993. 9p.
This human rights report describes and criticizes Ethiopian education policy under
both the Empire and the Derg.

280 **Traditional Ethiopian church education.**
Imbakom Kalewold, translated by Menghestu Lemma. New York:
Teachers College Press, 1970. 41p.
Constitutes an excellent introduction to the educational system and practices
traditionally found in highland Eritrea. A more Arab-Muslim-influenced Koranic
education was and is the norm in lowland and coastal Eritrea.

281 **Eritrea's university in a post-war era.**
Robin Lubbock. *The Chronicle of Higher Education*, vol. 40, no. 9 (20 October 1993), p. A55.
In this article Lubbock announced the closure of Eritrea's only university, the University of Asmara, as of October 1993. Insufficient staff and resources were cited as the reason. Hopes remained that Eritreans abroad would return to provide the country with a larger professional class and the university was operating once more by Spring 1995.

282 **Education in Ethiopia: prospect and retrospect.**
Teshome Wagaw. Ann Arbor, Michigan: University of Michigan Press, 1979. 256p. bibliog.
The development and future prospects of modern, Western-style education in Ethiopia and Eritrea is the subject of this book. It contains a lengthy and excellent bibliography (p. 217-51) and much material not widely available elsewhere.

Emergent Eritrea.
See item no. 256.

Literature

283 **Riding the whirlwind.**
Bereket Habte Selassie.   Trenton, New Jersey: Red Sea Press, 1993.
331p.
A work of historical fiction set in the homeland of this Eritrean author.

284 **To Asmara.**
Thomas Keneally.   New York: Warner Books, 1989. 290p.
A historical fiction set at the end of the Eritrean war for independence.

A Tigrinya chrestomathy.
See item no. 162.

Art, Music and Architecture

285 **Music in the Coptic church of Egypt and Ethiopia.**
John P. Bennett. Unpublished MA thesis, University of Washington, Seattle, Washington, 1945. 84p.
Probably the best scholarly source on the Coptic religious music found in highland Eritrea, this thesis includes a short bibliography, some illustrations and a good selection of music.

286 **Building power: Italy's colonial architecture and urbanism, 1923-1940.**
Mia Fuller. *Cultural Anthropology*, vol. 3, no. 4 (Autumn 1988), p. 455-87.
This special issue of *Cultural Anthropology* deals with Italian architecture in colonial Eritrea. It is one of the best presentations to be written on this topic.

287 **Churches in rock: early Christian art in Ethiopia.**
George Gerster, translated from the German by Richard Hosking.
London: Phaidon, 1970. 148p.
Rock-hewn churches in Ethiopia and early Christian art in both Eritrea and Ethiopia are described in this impressive work which contains numerous illustrations, contributions by David R. Buxton and a preface by Ethiopian Emperor Haile Selassie. A bibliography is included (p. 144-46).

288 **Wax and gold: tradition and innovation in Ethiopian culture.**
Donald N. Levine. Chicago: University of Chicago Press, 1970. 315p.
An illustrated description of the creative traditions of the Abyssinian highlands is presented in this scholarly book.

289 **Religious art of Ethiopia.**
Mammo Tessema, Richard Pankhurst, S. Chojnacki. Stuttgart:
Institut für Auslandsbeziehunger, 1973. 324p.

The art and symbolism of the Ethiopian Coptic Orthodox religious tradition is well
treated by this volume, which includes both colour and black-and-white illustrations
and photographs. The text is produced in both English and German. A great deal of
this material is applicable to highland Eritreans who have played ancient and
significant parts in this tradition.

290 **Rassegna.** (Review).
Bologna: 1979-present. quarterly.

This Italian architectural review publishes articles in Italian with summaries in
English, French and German. Volume 14, number 51 in September 1992 contained an
examination of the development of Italian military outposts in Eritrea during the late
19th century, of which one of the best sources is the article 'At the origins of the
Italian colonial politics: the illusion of conquest' by Fabrizio I. Appolonio (p. 6-15).
This piece also includes maps, photographs, models, site plans and a bibliography.
Appearing in the same issue is a good article on city planning in Eritrea under the
Italians: 'Eritrea: the first settlements' by Stefano Zagnoni & Giuliano Gresleri
(p. 28-35).

Travels in Ethiopia.
See item no. 31.

Coins and Stamps

291 **Experiencing Eritrea.**
Frank Correl. *The American Philatelist* (November 1993), p. 1,024.
Correl offers a good, brief study of Eritrea's postal history and current activities.

292 **The coinage of Ethiopia, Eritrea and Italian Somalia.**
Dennis Gill. Garden City, New York: Dennis Gill, 1990. 342p.
bibliog.
This is a well-illustrated guide to the coins, medals and banknotes of the Horn of Africa from Aksumite times to the present. Further information on Ethiopian coinage (circulated in Eritrea) was published by John Lenker in *Calcoin News*, the journal of the California State Numismatics Association, throughout 1975-76.

Biographies

293 The gentleman savage.
Sir Duncun Cummings.   London: Century, 1987. 176p. maps. bibliog.
Mansfield Parkyns (1823-94) left a privileged life in the English Midlands to travel through Egypt, the Sudan, Ethiopia and Eritrea. Settling in a village in North central Ethiopia, he lived among the local people, married a local woman, took part in raids on other villages and became very much a part of the community. Lady Palmerston described this as 'the most successful attempt by a man to reduce himself to the savage state on record'. Parkyns himself sought a level of understanding not often evident among Victorians. Maps, illustrations and a good bibliography are included in this account of his life.

294 Ethiopia and Eritrea during the scramble for Africa: a political biography of Ras Alula (1875-1897).
Haggai Erlikh.   East Lansing, Michigan: Michigan State University Press, 1982. 221p. bibliog.
A detailed look at Eritrean and Ethiopian history from 1490 to 1974 is provided within this biography of Ras Alula ([1847]-97). Ethiopian rulers and European colonialism are particularly well covered. This book was jointly produced by Michigan State University's African Studies Center (as monograph number eleven of its Ethiopian series) and by the Shiloah Center for Middle Eastern Studies in Tel Aviv, Israel. A good bibliography appears on pages 207 to 212.

295 The life and correspondence of Henry Salt.
J. J. Halls.   London: R. Bentley, 1834. 2 vols.
Salt's voyages to Eritrea in 1805 and 1809 feature in this biography, which concentrates mainly on his time in Egypt.

296 **Werner Münzinger Pascha: sein Leben und Wirken.** (Werner
Münzinger Pasha: his life and work).
J. V. Keller-Zschokke. Aarau, Switzerland: 1891.

This rare German-language biography of Werner von Münzinger is the only full-
length work on the Swiss trader/Egyptian governor. A good full-length treatment of
this important and interesting character remains to be written in English.

297 **Ventidue anni in Etiopia.** (Twenty-two years in Ethiopia).
Enrico Lucatello. Rome: Annali della Missione, 1936. 242p. bibliog.

The missionary work of Saint Justin of Jacobis in Eritrea has been the subject of a
number of books. This illustrated volume has a preface by Piero Bargellini and also
includes a short bibliography. An earlier biography is *Storia della vita del venerabile
Giustino de Jacobis, apostolo dell'Abissinia* (The story of the venerable Justin of
Jacobis, apostolo to Abyssinia) by D. d'Agostini (Naples: 1910). *Le vénerable Justin
de Jacobis* (The venerable Justin of Jacobis), a similar French-language biography of
Justin of Jacobis by G. Larigaldie, was published in Paris in 1910. Another shorter
work in Italian is *L'apostolo dell'Etiopia* (Apostle to Ethiopia) by Francesco Sirito
(Alba, Italy: Pia Societa san Paolo, 1941).

298 **Chi è? dell'Eritrea.** (Who's who in Eritrea?).
Giuseppe Puglisi. Asmara: Agenzia Regina, 1952. 304p.

This biographical dictionary with a chronology is the best available reference to the
leading personalities in Eritrea of the Italian era.

A handbook on Eritrea.
See item no. 6.

The Suma oriental of Tome Pires.
See item no. 10.

A voyage to Abyssinia.
See item no. 14.

The Periplus of the Erythraean Sea.
See item no. 16.

Ost-Africanische Studien. (East Africa Studies).
See item no. 23.

A voyage to Abyssinia and travels into the interior of that country.
See item no. 27.

**Voyages and travels to India, Ceylon, the Red Sea, Abyssinia and Egypt
in the years 1802-1806.**
See item no. 29.

A painful season/a stubborn hope.
See item no. 186.

Mass Media

299   **Africa Confidential.**
London: Miramoor Publications, January 1960-present. semi-monthly.
This semi-monthly newsletter has published excellent research carried out on the background and details behind African political news. A significant amount of material pertaining to Eritrea appears regularly and is often of a unique nature.

300   **Africa Report.**
New York: African-American Institute, July 1956-present. monthly.
As the African-American Institute's magazine, this monthly publication has presented African affairs in a consistently readable manner since the first sub-Saharan nations gained their independence from European colonial powers. Issues which have appeared around important events in Eritrea have contained in-depth articles on the country. They include 'Background to the Eritrea conflict' by J. F. Campbell (April 1970); 'Battle for the Red Sea' by Peter Robbs (February 1975); 'Who controls Ethiopia's destiny after Mengistu?' (July/August 1991); 'Beginning again' by Herbert Lewis (September/October 1991); 'Eritrea: breaking away' by Cameron McWhirter and Gur Melamede (November/December 1992); 'Eritrea votes to become Africa's newest nation' (May/June 1993); 'Birth of a nation' and 'The city on the High Plateau' both by Peter Biles (July/August 1993); and 'Getting all the help they can' by Sarah Gauch (July/August 1993).

301   **Africa Today.**
New York: 1953-present. quarterly.
A large number of short pieces on Eritrea have appeared in this journal surveying current events in Africa. The most important ones have been 'The OAU and regional conflicts: focus on the Eritrean War' by Bereket Habte Selassie (vol. 35, no. 3 [1988]); 'Eritrea through corrective lenses' an insightful review by Ruth Iyob (vol. 37, no. 4 [1990]); 'Environment and development in Eritrea' by Scott Jones (vol. 38, no. 2 [1991]); 'Eritrea and the United Nations' by James Abdel-Aziz (vol. 38, no. 2 [1991]); 'Eritrea and Ethiopia: strategies for reconciliation in the Horn'

by Roy Pateman (vol. 38, no. 2 [1991]); 'Eritrea: the socio-economic challenge of independence' by Araia Tseggai (vol. 38, no. 2 [1991]); 'Eritrean self-determination revisited' by Edmond Keller (vol. 38, no. 2 [1991]); 'Political mobilization and nationalist movements: the case of the Eritrean People's Liberation Front' by Tekle Mariam Woldemikael (vol. 38, no. 2 [1991]); 'A compelling analysis of the Eritrean struggle' by Amare Tekle (vol. 38, no. 2 [1991]); 'Eritrea: an emerging new nation in Africa's troubled Horn' by Roy Pateman (vol. 38, no. 2 [1991]); 'The Eritrean referendum overseas' by Edward Hawley (vol. 40, no. 2 [1993]); and 'Free Eritrea: lynchpin for stability and peace on the Horn' by George W. Shepherd (vol. 40, no. 2 [1993]).

302   The Economist.
London: 1843-present. fortnightly.

This British news magazine orientated toward business has published a surprisingly high number of articles on Eritrea. Recent ones include 'Ethiopia, Eritrea, Hunger' (24 February 1990, p. 40); 'Shaping up Eritrea' and 'An unborn nation' (both 20 October 1990, p. 50); 'Falling apart' (8 June 1991, p. 44-45); 'Morning in Ethiopia' (14 September 1991, p. 45); 'Squeezed' (12 October 1991, p. 44); 'Coming soon: Coca-Cola' (7 December 1991, p. 47-48); 'Freedom at last in Eritrea' (7 December 1991, p. 47); 'The Horn of Africa: dying and toying with maps' (10 October 1992, p. 50-53); 'Onions, potatoes and T-54s' (20 March 1993, p. 78) on the country's economic and political prospects; 'Another country' (24 April 1993, p. 20); 'Hungry again' (4 December 1993, p. 70) on crop failures in 1993; and 'The kitchen calls' (25 June 1994, p. 64) on the position of women.

303   Eritrea Information.
Rome: Research and Information Centre on Eritrea, 1979-88. monthly.

This newsletter was published by the Research and Information Centre on Eritrea (RICE) which was affiliated with the Eritrean People's Liberation Front (EPLF). A similar publication, *Eritrea in Struggle* (New York: Eritreans for Liberation in North America, 1976-91) was the North American newsletter of EPLF supporters.

304   Esploratore Commerciale. (Commercial Exploration).
Rome: 1886-? annual.

This Italian journal published some interesting early pieces on Eritrea, such as Pippo Vigoni on Keren and Sanhit in vol. 2 (1887); Enrico Tagliabue's account of a trip from Massawa to Keren in vol. 4 (1889); and Ottorino Rosa's letter (dated 21 August 1901) from Asmara in vol. 16 (1901).

305   The Ethiopia Observer.
Addis Ababa: 1956-74. quarterly.

A continuation of the *Ethiopia News and New Times*, which was edited by Sylvia Pankhurst and published in London from May 1936 until May 1956. Firmly Ethiopian unionist, the publication contained much news either on or related to Eritrea. One of numerous publications closed as a result of the Ethiopian Revolution, *The Ethiopia Observer* was a general periodical on Ethiopian culture, politics, geography, history and society. A number of interesting articles by Richard and Sylvia Pankhurst on agriculture were published in the late 1950s. Throughout 1959, Sylvia Pankhurst also wrote and edited several special issues on Eritrea (vol. 3, nos. 5, 6, 7 & 8). Several speeches on Eritrea by Emperor Haile Selassie were reproduced in the periodical throughout 1963. 'The foundations of education, printing, newspapers, book production, libraries and literacy in Ethiopia' by Richard Pankhurst (vol. 6 [1962], p. 241-90) is an excellent article with many applications to Eritrea. Articles on Red Sea ports were written by Richard Pankhurst (vol. 8, no. 1 [January 1964]) and Seyoum Tegegn Worq (vol. 12, no. 4 [October 1969], p. 242-43). Also good is David Hamilton's article on Ethiopia's boundary agreements in vol. 16, no. 2 (1973). Since August 1992, *The Addis Observer*, a similar periodical based in the Ethiopian capital has been published monthly.

306 **Hadas Eritrea.** (New Eritrea).
Asmara: 1991-present. twice weekly.

This newspaper is published by the Eritrean government in both the Tigrinya and Arabic languages. With a circulation of around 25,000, it represents the principal media in Eritrea after the official radio station. The Asmara Chamber of Commerce also publishes the newsletter *Chamber News* and the monthly *Trade and Development Bulletin*, both in Tigrinya and English. Prior to 1991, the few publications that circulated in Eritrea were Ethiopian-run. In addition to those mentioned elsewhere in this section: *The Daily News Bulletin* started in 1941, was printed by the Ministry of Information in French and English and was circulated primarily to foreign embassies up to 1974. The English-language daily, *Ethiopian Herald*, which started in 1945, was the main news source for the foreign community on government activities. Its editor was Tegenye Yeteshewerq, a Boston University graduate, who was executed by the Derg in November 1974 for suggesting moderation. Founded in 1941, *Rassegna di Studi Etiopici* (Ethiopian Studies Review) is the oldest scholarly journal in Ethiopia. In Eritrea itself, two Italian-language papers *Giornale dell'Eritrea* and *Il Quatidiano Eritreo* were published in Asmara and *xiSandek Alamtchin* (Our Flag), *Hebret*, and *xiAndnet* were published in Tigrinya, Arabic and Amharic.

307 **Index on Censorship.**
London: PEN International, 1971-present. monthly.

PEN International is a human rights organization for writers and journalists. This is their monthly magazine which has frequently contained news about censorship and other human rights violations in Eritrea. A history of the press in Eritrea is provided in 'A press in the making' by Ghirmai Negash (April 1993), p. 30-31.

308 **Jeune Afrique.** (Young Africa.)
Paris: 1961-present. monthly.

Some important past articles on Eritrea in this left-wing French magazine of African affairs are 'Mengistu au bord du gouffre' (Mengistu at the edge of the abyss) (17 April 1991, p. 29-31); and 'Independance' (Independence) (20 May 1993, p. 60-66) both by Marc Yared; and also Rene Guynnet's 'Erythree: du pain sur la planche (Eritrea: bread on the table) (28 July 1994, p. 24-25).

309 **New African.**
London: IC Publications, 1966-present. monthly.

This British-based colour magazine on Africa has featured numerous short articles on Eritrea. Some recent examples are: 'Ethiopia in turmoil' (July 1989), p. 9; 'Eritrea: independence beckons' (April 1990), p. 13; 'Eritrea: freedom at last' (November

322 Eritrea.
Historical Section of the Foreign Office. In: *Spanish and Italian African possessions and independent states.* London: HMSO, 1920. Reprinted, New York: Greenwood Press, 1969, vol. 20, no. 125. 60p. bibliog.

This handbook, prepared by the British Foreign Office and also reprinted in 1969 by Greenwood Press of New York, offers a comprehensive review of post-First World War Eritrea. Chapters include information, facts and statistics on physical and political geography, political history, social and political conditions and economic conditions. Appendices provide extracts from treaties and pre-First World War foreign trade statistics.

323 Eritrea.
Miles Smith-Morris, David Pool. In: *Africa South of the Sahara.* London: Europa Publications, 1994-present. annual. bibliog.

Entries in this authoritative annual (which has been in circulation since 1970) are divided into a number of sections beginning with essays on physical and social geography, recent history and the economy, written by a leading expert on the particular country covered. These background pieces are followed by a survey of area, population, economic, transport and education statistics and a directory which describes the country's constitution, government, legislature, political organizations, diplomatic representation, courts, religious institutions, the mass media, finance, trade and industry and transport. This data is accompanied by appropriate names and addresses. Each entry ends with a short bibliography. Good entries on independent Eritrea appear with the 1994 issue and after. As a new nation with rather hazy statistical records, historically and currently, Eritrea's entry is at present only four pages long (p. 347-50). However, an enormous amount of information is concentrated in this limited space.

324 A historical dictionary of Ethiopia and Eritrea.
Chris Prouty, Eugene Rosenfeld. Metuchen, New Jersey: Scarecrow, 1994. 614p. bibliog.

Part of Scarecrow's African Historical Dictionaries series (no. 32), this recent reference work on both Eritrea and Ethiopia is useful. It contains much information not found elsewhere in English, although its format is sometimes misleading. Despite the fact that it is described as a historical dictionary, this book contains a large amount of geographical, biographical and economic data and an extremely long bibliography (p. 345-612).

325 Horn of Africa.
Summit, New Jersey: 1978-present. quarterly.

This specialized journal of events in Eritrea, Ethiopia, Somalia, Djibouti and the Sudan has published various articles on Eritrea, including: 'The Eritrean struggle for independence and national liberation' by Tekle Fessehatzion (vol. 1, no. 2 [April 1978]); 'Eritrea: a survey of social and economic change' by Richard Sherman (vol. 1, no. 3 [July 1978]); 'Children's revolution: a bloodbath in Ethiopia' by Donald R. Katz (vol. 1, no. 3 [July 1978], p. 3-11); 'Eritrea: the politics of refugees' by Dan Connell (vol. 2, no. 4 [October 1979], p. 4-7); and 'An historical introduction to

1991), p. 21; 'Eritrea: building a new economy' (November 1991), p. 32; 'Eritrea's free press' (January 1992), p. 18; 'UN fails Eritrean refugees' (June 1992), p. 27-28; 'Eritrea: what next?' (December 1992), p. 40; 'Eritrea: ready for referendum' (March 1993), p. 20; 'Eritrea/Ethiopia: Israel's new African allies' (April 1993), p. 16; 'Eritrea's drive for economic revival' (May 1993), p. 31-32; 'Tribalism rules in Ethiopia' (September 1993), p. 20-21; 'Eritrea: troublesome new boy at the OAU' (September 1993), p. 38; 'Eritrea: enemies emerge' (April 1994), p. 31; and 'Eritrea gets its first bishops' (October 1994), p. 36.

310 New Statesman and Society.
London: 1988-present. weekly.

Some recent articles on Eritrea in this British magazine of liberal/leftist views are John Pilger's 'Horn of hope' and Amrit Wilson's 'Socialism from below' (both 7 June 1991) and Julie Wheelwright's two articles: 'Letter from Eritrea' (21 May 1993) and 'Eritrea's new dawn' (23 April 1993).

311 New Internationalist.
Oxford: 1973-present. monthly.

Some interesting articles on post-independence Eritrea were published in this British magazine. Among them are 'A traveller's notebook: the editor hits the road in Eritrea and Tigray' (1 December 1992); 'Native stranger' by Elsa Gebreyesus (1 December 1992) on women in post-independence Eritrea; and 'Ghebre's return' (1 December 1992) which describes the homecoming of a refugee.

312 The World Today.
London: Oxford University Press, 1945-present. monthly.

Published by Oxford University Press, this review of 20th-century history and politics has included Eritrea in its reportage. The wisdom of seeking federal solutions to the problems of Eritrea, Ethiopia and North-east Africa in general is questioned in the most important article on Eritrean politics published by *The World Today*: 'Another Ethiopian-Eritrean federation: an Eritrean view' by Amare Tekle (vol 47, no. 3 [March 1991]), p. 47-50.

Reference Works and Scholarly Journals

313 Abba Salama.

Athens: 1970-79. annual.

Abba Salama was the journal of the Association of Ethio-Hellenic Studies. Containing a great deal of material on Eritrea, the journal was devoted to research on Greek-Ethiopian connections. Its first editor was the former Metropolitan of the Greek church in Aksum, Methodios Fouyas. Articles are written in English with some text in Amharic or Greek. One good example of this journal's work is 'Reflections on the importance of Graeco-Ethiopian studies' by Richard Pankhurst (vol. 8, 1977).

314 Africa Affairs.

London: 1901-present. quarterly.

Recent coverage of Eritrea in the journal of the Royal African Society has included: 'Eritrea: historiography and mythology' by Patrick Gilkes (vol. 90, no. 361 [October 1991], p. 623-29); and 'Eritrean independence: the legacy of the Derg and the politics of reconstruction' by David Pool (vol. 92, no. 368 [July 1993], p. 389-403).

315 Africa Contemporary Record.

Edited by Colin Legum. London: Rex Collings; New York: Africana, 1970-present. annual.

The Eritrea entries in the recent volumes of this authoritative annual (1993 to the present) provide a continuous record of events, personalities, policies and issues of the country.

316 Africa Italiana. (Italian Africa).

Bergamo, Italy: 1927-41. quarterly.

This review of history and art in Italian Africa fell prey to the instability of its time and was suspended from 1936 to 1939.

317 Ausland.

Stuttgart: 1828-93. annual.

This German-language journal was eventually absorbed by *Globus*. Articles related to Eritrea included a piece by ship captain Albert Rodatz on his journey to Eritrea in the early 1840s (vol. 19 [1846]); and that of Johannes Rodatz on a 1847 journey in Eritrea in vol. 22 (1849).

318 Azania.

Nairobi: 1966-present. annual.

This is the journal of the British Institute of History and Archaeology in East Africa. One interesting article related to Eritrea was 'Gabata and other board games of Ethiopia and the Horn of Africa' by Richard Pankhurst in vol. 17 (1982, p. 27-42). Research into petroglyphs in Eritrea is described in 'Archaeological and environmental observations in Rora Habab, Eritrea' by Scott Jones in vol. 26 (1991, p. 5-11).

319 Bollettino della Società Africana d'Italia. (Bulletin of the Italian African Society).

Naples: 1882-1912. monthly.

Originally entitled *Africa*, this journal was continued by *L'Africa Italiana*. Included were: 'Obok ed Assab' (Obok and Assab) by G. B. Licata in vol. 1 (1882), p. 1-23; articles on Keren and Zula by G. Riola in vol. 7 (1888); a piece on Schweinfurth in Eritrea in vol. 10 (1891); V. Romano Scotti's 'Nell Eritrea inesplorata' (In unexplored Eritrea) in vol. 19 (1900); 'La legge sulla Colonia Eritrea al Senato' (vol. 21, 1902) (no author given); and 'Lo sviluppo commerciale della colonia Eritrea' (The commercial development of the colony of Eritrea) by D. Bartolotti (vol. 24, 1905). *L'Africa Italiana* (Italian Africa) (Naples: 1913-37. monthly), the successor to the *Bollettino della Società Africana d'Italia*, carried a good piece by G. Paladino 'Documenti per la storia della colonia Eritrea' (Historical documents on the Eritrea colony) (vol. 37, 1918).

320 Bollettino della Società Geografica d'Italia. (Bulletin of the Italian Geographical Society).

Rome: 1868-present. monthly.

A number of interesting articles have been published in this journal which has appeared in eight different formats and numberings. The most important for those studying Eritrea are: 'Relazione sommaria del viaggio nel Mar Rosso' (Summarized report on a journey on the Red Sea) by M. Amadeo, O. Beccari and A. Issel in vol. 5 (1870); 'Da Massaua a Chartum per Keren e Cassala' (From Massawa to Khartoum via Keren and Kassala) by L. Gatta in vol. 22 (1885); Leopoldo Traversi's articles on the Danakil in vol. 23 (1886), p. 516-27 and vol. 30 (1893), p. 105-08; and 'Una cucina barbara: come mangiano gli Abissini d'Eritrea' (A barbaric cuisine: how the Abyssinians eat Eritrea) by A. M. Tancredi in vol. 44 (1907).

321 Current History.

New York: 1915-present. monthly.

The two best articles to cover Eritrea in this American current affairs monthly have been 'Nationalism and separatism in East Africa' by Kenneth W. Grundy (vol. 54, 1968) and 'Eritrea takes the world stage' by Roy Pateman (vol. 93, May 1994).

refugee problems in the Horn' by Richard Greenfield (vol. 2, no. 4 [October 1979], p. 14-26).

326 **Journal of African History.**
Cambridge, England: Cambridge University Press, 1960-present. quarterly.
This prestigious journal has published a number of articles on Eritrean history and archaeology including Carlo Giglio's 'Article 17 of the Treaty of Uccialli' (vol. 6, no. 2 [April 1965]); W. Macgaffy's 'Concepts of race in the historiography of North East Africa' (vol. 7, no. 1 [January 1966]); Lloyd Ellingson's 'The emergence of political parties in Eritrea 1941-1950 (vol. 18, no. 2 [April 1977], p. 261-81); Merid W. Aregay's 'The early history of Ethiopia's coffee trade and the rise of Shawa' (vol. 29, no. 1 [January 1988], p. 19-25); and Friederike Kemink's 'Die Tegrenna Frauen in Eritrea' (Tigrinya women in Eritrea) (vol. 33, no. 3 [July 1992], p. 500).

327 **Journal of African Studies.**
Washington DC: 1974-present. quarterly.
Published by the African Studies Center at the University of California in Los Angeles (UCLA), this journal included articles such as 'Afar pastoralists in transition and the Ethiopian Revolution' by Teferra-Worq Beshah and John W. Harbeson (vol. 5, no. 2 [Summer 1978], p. 249-67).

328 **Journal of Ethiopian Studies.**
Addis Ababa: 1963-present. quarterly.
This journal has published many interesting articles on Eritrea in Amharic, English, French and Italian. The best of a lengthy list are: 'The trade of Northern Ethiopia in the 19th and early 20th centuries' by Richard Pankhurst in vol. 2, no. 1 (January 1964); 'War chants in praise of ancient Afar heroes' by Georges C. Savard in vol. 3, no. 1 (January 1965); 'The travels of Jerónimo Lobo' by C. F. Beckingham in vol. 4, no. 1 (1966), p. 1-4; 'A note to the list of the emperors of Ethiopia' by Elisabeth-Dorothea Hecht in vol. 7, no. 1 (January 1969); 'Aksumite influence on the Beja cult in the Middle Ages' by Fawzy Mikawy in vol. 12, no. 1 (1974), p. 183-84; 'The Eritrean problem revisited' by Negussay Ayele in vol. 22 (1989); 'Ethiopian plow agriculture in the nineteenth century' by Donald Crummey in vol. 16, no. 1 (1983), p. 1-23; 'Issues in language policy and language choice: a sociolinguistic profile of the major Ethiopian languages' by Takkele Taddese in vol. 18 (1985), p. 80-90; 'Peasant responses to famine in Ethiopia, 1975-1985' by Adhana Haile Adhana in vol. 21 (1988), p. 1-56; 'Food and development in Ethiopia: retrospect and prospect' by Fassil G. Kiros in vol. 21 (1988), p. 83-110; 'A new Axumite chronology' by R. Schneider in vol. 21 (1988), p. 111-20; and 'Some notes on the genesis and interpretation of the Tripartite Treaty' by Shiferaw Bekele in vol. 18 (1985), p. 63-79.

329 **Journal of Modern African Studies.**
London: 1963-present. quarterly.
Published by Cambridge University Press, this journal has featured a number of important articles on Eritrea, such as: 'The Revolution betrayed: Ethiopia 1974-9' by Michael Chege (vol. 17, no. 3 [September 1979], p. 359-80); 'The American dilemma on the Horn' by Bereket Habte Selassie (vol. 22, no. 2 [June 1984], p. 249-72);

'The Eritrean question: an alternative explanation' by Mesfin Araya (vol. 28, no. 1 [March 1990], p. 79); 'Liberté, egalité, fraternité: aspects of the Eritrean revolution' by Roy Pateman (vol. 28, no. 3 [September 1990], p. 457-65); 'Discourses on Eritrean nationalism and identity' by John Sorenson (vol. 29, no. 2 [June 1991], p. 301-20); an excellent analysis of the politics of famine and war in the Horn of Africa 'Drought, war and the politics of famine in Ethiopia and Eritrea' by Edmond J. Keller (vol. 30, no. 4 [December 1992], p. 609-24); and 'Regional hegemony: domination and resistance in the Horn of Africa' by Ruth Iyob (vol. 31, no. 2 [June 1993] p. 257-77).

330 Paideuma.

Stuttgart: 1955-present. annual.

This cultural journal has published articles on Eritrea in German, English and French. They include: 'L'archeologie d'Axoum en 1972' (The archaeology of Aksum in 1972) by Francis Anfray in vol. 18 (1972), p. 60-78; 'Herrschaft und Reich in Athiopien: Politische Anthropologie und Verfassungsrechts' (Power and Empire in Ethiopia: political anthropology and constitutional law) by Heinrich Scholler in vol. 35 (1989), p. 247-56; 'Bar Zaf: l'eucalyptus en Ethiopie' (The Eucalyptus in Ethiopia) by Joseph Tubiana in vol. 36 (1990), p 329-33; and 'Tegrenna customary law codes' by Friederike Kemink in vol. 37 (1991), p. 55-72.

331 Proceedings of the Third International Conference on Ethiopian Studies.

Addis Ababa: Addis Ababa University Press, 1969. 329p.

Papers presented at this conference include 'Church and state in the Aksumite period' by Sergew Haile Selassie; 'Jeronimo Lobo reveals Ethiopia to Europe in the middle of the XVIIth century' by Manuel Da Costa; 'Primitivo stanziamento estra eritreo dei Cunama' (Eritrean primitive findings of the Kunama) by M. Cittadini; and 'Cross cousin marriage among the patrilineal Afar' by Georges C. Savard; 'Note storiche sulle isole Dahlac' (Historical notes on the Dahlak islands) by S. Tedeschi.

332 Proceedings of the Fifth International Conference on Ethiopian Studies.

Edited by Robert L. Hess.   Chicago: University of Illinois Press, 1979. 829p.

Much of the work presented at this conference was related to Eritrea, either directly or indirectly. The most relevant papers, which were presented and subsequently published, were 'The Islamic Red Sea slave trade: an effort at quantification' by Ralph Austen; 'Civil-military elite interaction in the Ethiopian Revolution: the role of students' by Marilyn Baissa; 'Land tenure: the underlying cause of the Ethiopian Revolution' by Lapiso D. Dilebo; 'The origins and development of the Eritrean Liberation Movement' by Lloyd Ellingson; 'The establishment of the Derg: the turning of a protest movement into a Revolution' by Haggai Erlich; 'Toward a political theory of the Ethiopian Revolution' by John W. Harbeson; 'Remarks on the Ethiopian Revolution: a personal view' by Getatchew Mekasha; 'Ethiopian opposition to Italian Rule 1936-1940' by Alberto Sbacchi; and 'Ethiopia: human rights 1948-1978' by Norman J. Singer.

333 **Review of African Political Economy.**

London: 1974-present. quarterly.

This British journal has provided good recent articles on the situation in Eritrea. The best have included: 'Revolutionary crisis and revolutionary vanguard: the emergence of the Eritrean People's Liberation Front' by David Pool (September-December 1980), p. 33-47; 'The Ethiopian military state and Soviet-US Involvement in the Horn of Africa' by James F. Petras (September 1984), p. 21-31; 'Nationalism, peasant politics and the emergence of a vanguard front in Eritrea' by Jordan Gebre-Medhin (September 1984), p. 48-57; 'Eritrea: a country in transition' by Okbazghi Yohannes (July 1993), p. 7-28; 'Eritrea: birth of a nation (July 1993), p. 110; 'Eritrea: the transitional period' by John Markakis (November 1993), p. 131; and 'The formation and recognition of new states: Somaliland in contrast to Eritrea' by Hussein M. Adam (March 1994), p. 21-38.

Bibliographies

334 **Bibliografia Etiopica.** (Ethiopian bibliography).
Giuseppe Fumagalli.   Milan: Ulrico Hoepli, 1893. 288p.
Fumagalli included 2,758 entries in this, one of the earliest bibliographies on Ethiopia. Section K on the history of the Italian colony of Eritrea is particularly rich in rare titles.

335 **Ethiopia and the Italo-Ethiopian conflict.**
D. C. Haskell.   New York: New York Public Library, 1936. 13p.
Reprinted from the January 1936 issue of the *Bulletin of the New York Public Library*, this short bibliography is a good starting point for those researching Eritrea in the 1930s, but is of limited use to advanced scholars. Better, but difficult to acquire, is Richard Pankhurst's *A provisional bibliography on the Italian Invasion and occupation and the liberation of Ethiopia – 1935-1941* (Addis Ababa: [n.p.], 1972. 68p.)

336 **Africa bibliography series: Northeast Africa.**
Ruth Jones.   London: International African Institute, 1959. 51p.
General works and specific sources on Eritrean ethnography, sociology and linguistics are included in this useful volume.

337 **The modern history of Ethiopia and the Horn of Africa: a select and annotated bibliography.**
Harold G. Marcus.   Palo Alto, California: Hoover Institution Press, 1972. 641p.
This is the best of a number of bibliographies of Ethiopia, which prominently feature Eritrea. Another is *Ethiopian perspectives: a bibliographical guide to the history of Ethiopia* by Clifton F. Brown (Westport, Connecticut: Greenwood, 1978. 264p.). An earlier reference collection is *A study guide for Ethiopia and the Horn of Africa* by John Sommer of the African Studies Center at Boston University (Boston: Boston

University Press, 1969. 94p.). Daniel G. Matthews' *A current bibliography on Ethiopian affairs: a select bibliography from 1950-1964* (Washington DC: African Bibliographic Center, 1965. 46p.) is the third volume of ten in a series on African topics and was reprinted by the Negro Universities Press in New York in 1969. Earlier still is the unattributed *Ethiopia 1950-1962: a select bibliography* (Washington DC: Africa House, 1963. 32p.). This short bibliography is particularly good on politics, the political economy, treaties, diplomacy, trade unions, foreign aid and technical assistance. It was reprinted in New York in 1968 by the Negro Universities Press. Also of some use is *The United States and Africa: a guide to U. S. official documents and government sponsored publications 1785-1975* by Julian W. Witherell (Washington DC: Library of Congress, 1978. 949p.), which contains some sources on the history of US-Ethiopian and US-Eritrean relations. Several official Ethiopian bibliographies are also useful in Eritrean studies: *A bibliography of Ethiopia* (Addis Ababa: Ministry of Foreign Affairs, 1968. 46p.) and Pamela Bell's *Land tenure in Ethiopia: a bibliography* (Addis Ababa: Haile Selassie University Library, 1968. 25p.). An interesting reference book containing a great deal on Eritrea is *A Soviet view of Africa: an annotated bibliography on Ethiopia, Somalia and Djibouti* by Colin Darch (Boston, Massachusetts: G. K. Hall, 1980. 200p.).

338 **Red Sea, Gulf of Aden and Suez Canal: a bibliography on oceanographic and marine environmental research.**
Edited by Selim A. Morcos, Allen Varley. Paris: UNESCO; Jeddah: Alecso-Persga, 1990. 48p. map.

This bibliographical reference to Red Sea oceanography and marine biology was compiled by A. A. Banaja, A. I. Beltagy and M. A. Zahran, with a scientific contribution by M. K. El-Sayed. The work consists of texts in English and Arabic with one folded leaf of plates and a colour map.

339 **Bibliography on Eritrea.**
Research and Information Centre on Eritrea. Rome: RICE, 1982. 235p.

This collection of 3,376 sources was gathered by Eritrean exile organizations. It is one of the few full-length general bibliographies devoted solely to Eritrea. One earlier bibliographical article is *Eritrea: a preliminary bibliography* by Kassahun Checole (*Africana Journal*, vol. 6, no. 4 [1975]).

340 **Piccola bibliografia dell'Africa orientale con speciale riguardo all'Eritrea e paesi confianti.** (A short bibliography on East Africa with special regard to Eritrea and the surrounding countries).
Alberto Pollera. Asmara: Tip. Coloniale Ditta M. Fioritti, 1933. 61p.

Produced for the Italian colonial government in Eritrea, Pollera's work is an excellent bibliography of Italian sources prior to the Mussolini era, in Italian. An English-language work covering this same era is *A bibliography of Italian colonization in Africa with a section on Abyssinia* by D. H. Yarley (Folkstone, England: Dawsons of Pall Mall, 1970).

341 **Bibliografia geologica Italiana per gli anni 1915-1933: Africa Orientale Italiana.** (Italian geological bibliography for the years 1915-1933: Italian East Africa).

Anonymous.   Rome: Istituto Poligrafico dello Stato, 1936. 166p.

Though dated, this collection of geological sources remains valuable.

Index

The index is a single alphabetical sequence of authors (personal and corporate), titles of publications and subjects. Index entries refer both to the main items and to other works mentioned in the notes to each item. Title entries are in italics. Numeration refers to the items as numbered.

113

114

Map of Eritrea

This map shows the more important towns and other features.

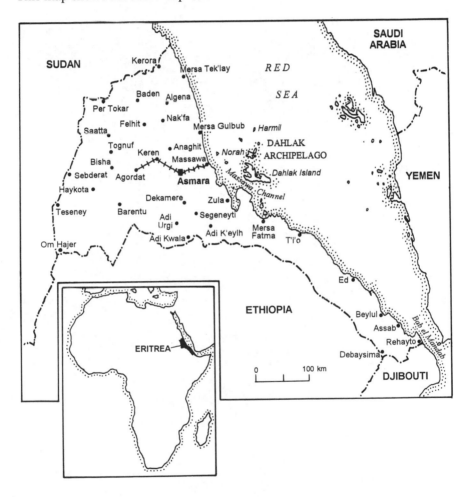

ALSO FROM CLIO PRESS

INTERNATIONAL ORGANIZATIONS SERIES

Each volume in the International Organizations Series is either devoted to one specific organization, or to a number of different organizations operating in a particular region, or engaged in a specific field of activity. The scope of the series is wide-ranging and includes intergovernmental organizations, international non-governmental organizations, and national bodies dealing with international issues. The series is aimed mainly at the English-speaker and each volume provides a selective, annotated, critical bibliography of the organization, or organizations, concerned. The bibliographies cover books, articles, pamphlets, directories, databases and theses and, wherever possible, attention is focused on material about the organizations rather than on the organizations' own publications. Notwithstanding this, the most important official publications, and guides to those publications, will be included. The views expressed in individual volumes, however, are not necessarily those of the publishers.

VOLUMES IN THE SERIES

1 *European Communities*, John Paxton
2 *Arab Regional Organizations*, Frank A. Clements
3 *Comecon: The Rise and Fall of an International Socialist Organization*, Jenny Brine
4 *International Monetary Fund*, Anne C. M. Salda
5 *The Commonwealth*, Patricia M. Larby and Harry Hannam

6 *The French Secret Services*, Martyn Cornick and Peter Morris
7 *Organization of African Unity*, Gordon Harris
8 *North Atlantic Treaty Organization*, Phil Williams
9 *World Bank*, Anne C. M. Salda
10 *United Nations System*, Joseph P. Baratta
11 *Organization of American States*, David Sheinin

TITLES IN PREPARATION

British Secret Services, Philip H. J. Davies

Israeli Secret Services, Frank A. Clements